D1557898

Civic Librarianship

Renewing the Social Mission of the Public Library

Ronald B. McCabe

The Scarecrow Press, Inc.
Lanham, Maryland, and London
2001

SCARECROW PRESS, INC.

Published in the United States of America
by Scarecrow Press, Inc.
4720 Boston Way, Lanham, Maryland 20706
www.scarecrowpress.com

4 Pleydell Gardens, Folkestone
Kent CT20 2DN, England

British Library Cataloguing-in-Publication Information Available

Library of Congress Cataloging-in-Publication Data

McCabe, Ronald B., 1948–
  Civic librarianship : renewing the social mission of the public library / Ronald B.
  McCabe.
    p. cm.
  Includes bibliographical references (p.) and index.
  ISBN 0-8108-3905-9 (alk. paper)
    1. Libraries and community—United States. 2. Public libraries—Social aspects—
United States. 3. Public libraries—Aims and objectives—United States. I. Title.

Z716.4 M38 2001
021.2'0973—dc21   2001020589

⊖™ The paper used in this publication meets the minimum requirements of
American National Standard for Information Sciences—Permanence of
Paper for Printed Library Materials, ANSI/NISO Z39.48-1992.
Manufactured in the United States of America.

To Deborah,
my partner in life and libraries

Contents

Foreword

I have been a librarian for over 30 years. I remember in the early 1980s when Charles Robinson, director of the Baltimore County Public Library, first advanced his "give 'em what they want" theory of book selection. In the past, librarians placed quality at the center of their book selection choices, purchasing books that were well reviewed and reflected a high level of quality. Robinson said that taxpayers should have the books they want rather than the books librarians select for them by whatever criteria. Robinson also had radical marketing ideas including the idea of using face-out or bookstore-type shelving as a way of marketing books. I was excited and empowered by his ideas. I went back to my library to put them into practice immediately.

In the late 1980s, on being appointed director of the Multnomah County Library in Portland, Oregon, I announced to the press that I would be "running the library like a business." Although the library did not have a profit and loss statement, I noted that we did have measures of our outputs. This was a concept that had just been developed by the Public Library Association, and I intended to use these measures in order to make the library more useful and accountable to the community. At the time, my comments were considered newsworthy and a fresh approach to library management.

Later when the Public Library Association issued *Planning and Role Setting for Public Libraries*, I eagerly followed the manual's process of utilizing a selected group of citizens and staff to choose among eight roles for each library in the system. The idea was that no library could possibly offer all the services in all eight roles. By focusing on a role or two or three that were then most relevant to the community, better service could be offered. In the early 1990s, with the advent of the Internet, I remember giving speeches and claiming proudly that libraries were in the "information business." I pointed to the fact that information came in many formats and that the library had all formats available and ready to use.

All of these ideas seemed appropriate at the time they were implemented. They seemed to advance the cause of public library service. An unintended consequence of adopting private-sector marketing strategies, however, was a movement away from the educational mission of the public library, which has been our foundation. Unwittingly we were fitting in with a tide of stylish opinion that was sweeping the country, opinion that was both anti-intellectual and anti-authority. We embraced the rights of the individual above all else and minimized the public library's claim to the traditional educational social mission. As Ron McCabe puts it, "In the wake of the cultural civil war of the 1960s, the public library's republican mission of education for a democratic society declined sharply under the challenge of a libertarian mission of access to information for individuals." Having seen the bigger picture, I agree with Ron McCabe. We must renew the social mission of the public library or lose our reason for being as well as our claim on local tax dollars.

When interviewed by a reporter from the *New York Times* several weeks ago, I was asked my opinion of the following criticism of a public library in the Midwest, "The library is just a tax-funded recreation center and not worthy of tax dollars." While most Americans still believe that the public library is at least related to education, those who look closely will see that we have lost our fire for asserting the authority of the public library's educational mission. Library trustees and directors and other spokespersons have failed to claim the higher authority and responsibility of the educational message. Again, in McCabe's words, "The voices of library leaders have been softened both by society's declining support for social authorities and public education and by personal doubts about the appropriateness of serving as educators, administrators, and leaders." It is easier to claim that the library is simply a reflection of the community that it serves than it is to assert a role of education and community leadership.

In 1998 when I was president-elect of the American Library Association, I was searching for a focus or a theme for my year as president. I talked to people, I read articles, I mulled it over. The baby boomers were turning 50. Many people were telecommuting or working from home. Starbucks and Kinko's were becoming gathering places as well as centers of commerce. People were longing for a place to come together as a community. As a librarian it was obvious to me that the library in a city, town, village, school, university, or business was the social and intellectual heart of whatever community it served. I made "Libraries Build Community" the theme for my year as president. I wanted to say to the library community, "You have always been involved in community building. Step it up. Do more. Reach out. Institute partnerships and alliances. Show that the library is a safe place for people to come together as it has always been a safe place for ideas, even conflicting ideas, to come together." In the same way I wanted to say to the general public, "Look to your library to be the heart of the community where you live, work, go to school. Expect the library and librarian to reach out to everyone in the community."

During this period, I talked to Ron McCabe. He was also feeling that there was a sea change in the offing for public libraries, but the focus of his thoughts was on the mission of the public library. So McCabe went off to research civic librarianship while I went off to be ALA president and to talk to librarians and the general public about the potential of the library to be a community-gathering place.

I wish I had had Ron McCabe's book earlier. His research marries the concept of the library as a community gathering place with the philosophy of education as the paramount societal mission of the library. He explains the cultural origins of the anti-intellectual, pro-individual philosophy that has swept our country since 1965. He shows how librarianship fits into this tide of radical individualism. This book connects the pieces of a very large puzzle by explaining why the "give 'em what they want" approach to book selection and the other private-sector strategies adopted over the last thirty years, although appropriate for their day, diluted the educational purpose of the library. He shows why it is appropriate and necessary *now* for public librarians to reach back to their roots and embrace the library's social mission of education for a democratic society.

This book will challenge your thinking about public libraries. It places librarianship in a broader societal context. It calls for the renewal of the public library's traditional social mission as the foundation for library development in the new century. Ron McCabe has given us a thoughtful philosophical treatise on public libraries in America. I commend his work to you.

Sarah Ann Long

Acknowledgments

I have discovered that even the solitary process of writing a book is a profoundly social activity. This book would not have been possible without the encouragement and the support of many people.

I want to thank Amitai Etzioni and the other great writers I have quoted here, Harland Nelson and the Luther College English Department for teaching me to write, and Scarecrow Press for supporting a first-time author with a big idea.

I also want to thank my library colleagues for their interest in these ideas and their encouragement. I am especially grateful to Sarah Ann Long, Nancy Kranich, Eleanor Jo Rodger, Frederick Schlipf, Richard Thompson, Sandra Norlin, Kathleen Balcom, Kay Runge, Faye Clow, Peter Hamon, John Nichols, Kenneth Hall, and Elizabeth Carreño Guedea. I have greatly appreciated the support of McMillan Memorial Library Board members Linda Vollert, William Lindroth, Charles Lester, James Quinn, Mary Jo Hane, Dean Ryerson, Larry Jorgenson, Clifford Starr, and Donna Smart. I am also grateful to Assistant Director Andrew Barnett and Business Office Manager Kathlene Gronski for their hard work during my leave of absence.

I thank my mother and father, Joyce and William McCabe, for their love. Most of all, I thank my wife Deborah whose emotional support, understanding of public libraries, and knowledge of word processing have been invaluable to me at every stage of this project.

Introduction

Jesse Shera once made the following assessment of the usefulness of studying library history:

> If future generations can learn anything from an examination of library history, it is that the objectives of the public library are directly dependent upon the objectives of society itself. The true frame of reference for the library is to be found in its coeval culture. No librarian can see clearly the ends which he should seek when his country is confused about the direction in which it is moving. When people are certain of the goals toward which they strive, the function of the public library can be precisely defined.[1]

The bad news for public libraries has been that Americans have been confused and deeply divided since the social conflict of the 1960s, a time that E. J. Dionne Jr. has described as America's "cultural civil war."[2] As the conflict over the impeachment of President Clinton demonstrated, cultural confusion and division continue to damage our national life. The good news is that a major cultural shift, referred to here as the *community movement*, has begun to unite Americans and to offer the clarity needed to achieve common goals. This emerging culture of healing offers hope for the nation and hope for librarians and trustees who need to clarify the mission of the public library for a new century of service.

Library leaders, like most Americans, are vaguely aware of the community movement. The ideas of this movement have transformed the Democratic Party in the United States and the Labour Party in Great Britain. This cultural shift has been described as a "third way" to approach social and political issues, a means of transcending cultural warfare and political gridlock. It may be observed in such efforts to strengthen communities as the following:

- discovering social and political common ground
- renewing a social morality that balances rights and responsibilities
- replacing argument with civility and dialogue
- collaborating to solve social problems
- strengthening the institutions of civil society
- stressing character development and civic education in public schools
- integrating law enforcement into neighborhood life through community policing
- restoring the democratic purpose of the press through civic journalism
- reexamining zoning laws and community planning to enhance civic life

A full discussion of the role libraries can play in building communities is now underway. Two consecutive presidents of the American Library Association have chosen presidential themes relating to the civic role of libraries. Sarah Ann Long chose "Libraries Build Community" for her presidential theme in 1999-2000; Nancy Kranich chose the theme "Libraries: The Cornerstone of Democracy" in 2000-2001. This discussion has also been advanced by the publication of *Civic Space/Cyberspace: The American Public Library in the Information Age* by Redmond Kathleen Molz and Phyllis Dain[3] and *A Place at the Table: Participating in Community Building* by Kathleen de la Peña McCook.[4]

Experiments in building communities through public library service have become increasingly visible thanks to highly successful efforts at libraries such as the Queens Borough Public Library, Brooklyn Public Library, Chicago Public Library, and a host of other libraries throughout the nation. These innovations have been encouraged by the Urban Libraries Council and the non-profit group Libraries for the Future. A recent *New York Times* article described the Queens Borough Public Library as being "at the forefront of a major shift at public libraries across the country" toward "finding ways to become more essential to the neighborhoods that surround them."[5]

This book is an attempt to deepen the discussion of community building by demonstrating how the ideas of the community movement can help librarians and trustees to develop more effective public libraries. Special attention will be given to the ideas of sociologist Amitai Etzioni and other writers who describe their views as *communitarian*. The communitarians have best articulated the social philosophy emerging from the community movement. They have also provided leadership in demonstrating the public policy implications of community movement ideas. The book's goal is to introduce librarians and trustees to a powerful new paradigm for library development that offers a fresh perspective on community building as well as a new approach to the perennial questions that face library leaders. This new paradigm is in many ways more in tune with the historical tradition of the public library than with the ideas that currently dominate public library development. As often happens, the journey to the future requires a reassessment of the past.

The book will begin with an examination of America's cultural civil war and its effect on public libraries. This discussion will be placed in the context of the history of the public library in America. A general description of community movement ideas will follow. *Civic librarianship* will then be defined in terms of the institutional reforms that this new approach makes possible. The book will conclude with an exploration of the implications that civic librarianship might have for specific professional concerns and an assessment of the importance of civic librarianship to the future of the public library.

Civic librarianship is at once a return to the best traditions of public library service and a new perspective capable of propelling the public library into the new century. Public librarians and trustees understand that theories of operation are useful only when they can be used to solve real world problems. The ideas that follow are passing the test of application every day as America's public libraries begin to find a new balance between service to individuals and service to the social structures that support individual life.

Notes

1. Jesse H. Shera, *Foundations of the Public Library: Origins of the Public Library Movement in New England 1629-1855* (Chicago: University of Chicago Press, 1949; n.p.: Shoe String Press, 1965), 248.

2. E. J. Dionne Jr., *Why Americans Hate Politics* (New York: Simon & Schuster, 1991), 11.

3. Redmond Kathleen Molz and Phyllis Dain, *Civic Space/Cyberspace: The American Public Library in the Information Age* (Cambridge, Mass.: MIT Press, 1999).

4. Kathleen de la Peña McCook, *A Place at the Table: Participating in Community Building* (Chicago and London: American Library Association, 2000).

5. Dean E. Murphy, "Moving Beyond 'Shh' (and Books) at Libraries," *New York Times*, 7 March 2001, East Coast late edition.

1

America's Cultural Civil War

In his 1991 book *Why Americans Hate Politics*, E. J. Dionne Jr. noted that the social conflicts of the 1960s continue to powerfully influence contemporary politics.

> We are suffering from a false polarization in our politics, in which liberals and conservatives keep arguing about the same things when the country wants to move on.
>
> The cause of this false polarization is the cultural civil war that broke out in the 1960s. Just as the Civil War dominated American political life for decades after it ended, so is the cultural civil war of the 1960s, with all its tensions and contradictions, shaping our politics today. We are still trapped in the 1960s.[1]

In a December 1998 article in the *Washington Post*, David Broder and Richard Morlin explain that, "The sharply divided public reaction to the impeachment of President Clinton has provided a dramatic showcase of a struggle for American values that goes back to the 1960s and remains unresolved today." They report that, "Some describe it as a battle of extremes—the Puritanism of the Religious Right vs. the permissiveness of the aging children of the '60s."[2]

It is clear that the divisions of America's cultural civil war have been slow to heal. These divisions *are* healing, however, thanks, in part, to the community movement's success in diagnosing the nature of this cultural conflict and offering an attractive alternative that synthesizes seemingly antagonistic social and political ideas. To understand the community movement's proposal for an end to the cultural war and an end to political gridlock, it is necessary to analyze the great American argument between Right and Left, an argument that crystallized in the 1960s, but one that has deep cultural roots.

In their 1985 book *Habits of the Heart: Individualism and Commitment in American Life*, Robert Bellah and his co-authors provide a useful model for American political culture. *Habits of the Heart* describes the three central strands of American culture as being "biblical, republican, and modern individualist" with two types of individualism, "utilitarian individualism" and "expressive individualism."[3] The biblical tradition is, of course, the moral perspective of the dominant American religions. The republican tradition is the civic tradition of American democracy that grew out of the philosophical ideas of the eighteenth-century Enlightenment. Utilitarian individualism refers to the tradition of personal economic freedom that has been the driving force behind American capitalism. Expressive individualism refers to a tradition that advocates freedom from the social constraints limiting personal expression. Expressive individualism was popularized by American writers who were influenced by Romanticism in the nineteenth century and by the cultural successors of Romanticism in the twentieth century. The biblical, republican, utilitarian individualist and expressive individualist cultural traditions have interacted for several hundred years. The recent cultural warfare has been among the most explosive of these interactions.

The cultural civil war of the 1960s was ignited by the tremendous surge in the popularity of expressive individualism that resulted from the emergence of the counterculture and its political wing the New Left. The counterculture rebelled against a dominant culture that was perceived to be narrowly rational and biased against the subjective reality of the individual. The dominant culture, often referred to as *the system* or *the establishment*, was thought to enforce an objective, social reality through the use of technology and social structures. This dominance by a socioeconomic elite was thought to be unfair to women, ethnic minorities, and the poor. The great domestic movement was the civil rights movement, which became a model for a proliferation of other rights movements as well as the environmental movement. The great international issue was the war in Vietnam. These movements, although very large, were spontaneous and loosely structured due to the counterculture's distrust of social organization and the role of leaders. Rock music was a primary means of communicating the values of the counterculture. Recreational drugs were popular, as was sexual activity outside marriage.

There is general, though obviously not universal, acceptance that the counterculture was right to address the negative traits of the dominant culture of the 1960s. At its best the counterculture was, like the work of Martin Luther King Jr., a search for a beloved community that would include and support all Americans. It has become increasingly obvious, however, that the counterculture's contribution to the present culture has been marred not only by lifestyle excesses but also by erroneous cultural assumptions borrowed from the expressive individualism of Romanticism.

Beginning in the 1960s, ideas that had been at the fringe of the culture suddenly presented a powerful challenge to the social morality of the biblical and republican traditions. The resulting cultural tension was complicated in the 1980s by the rise of the libertarian political philosophy, which can be viewed as an alliance between expressive individualism and utilitarian individualism. In the 1990s the community movement with its communitarian philosophy sought to renew the traditions of social morality in an effort to counter the extreme individualism of libertarian politics. This chapter will describe the ideas in conflict in America's cultural civil war of the 1960s and 1970s, the libertarian consensus of the 1980s, and the communitarian response to the libertarian consensus in the 1990s. Although underlying technological and social changes clearly influenced this conflict of ideas, the discussion here is limited to the level of social and political ideology. This background information will provide a framework for discussing the history of the public library and the usefulness of communitarian ideas to public library development.

Romanticism and the Historical War of Ideas

Most Americans have some understanding of the biblical and republican cultural traditions and everyone is aware of the powerful tradition of utilitarian individualism behind American capitalism. Very few Americans, however, understand the roots of the counterculture in Romanticism. The inability to understand the influence of counterculture Romanticism on the political Left and on the culture as a whole is an important reason why the cultural war is so difficult to resolve. This understanding is also critically important to studying the social context of educational and cultural institutions like the public library. Such institutions have been among the segments of American society most deeply influenced by the expressive individualism of Romanticism.

Romanticism: "The Big Bang of Modern Culture"

Although the counterculture is a relatively recent social phenomenon, the philosophy that the counterculture espoused is squarely within a much older tradition, the tradition of Romanticism, which began in the eighteenth century. Romanticism was a movement in the arts that had a powerful influence on the general culture of Europe and America. Major writers associated with Romanticism in England included Blake, Wordsworth, Coleridge, Byron, Shelley, Keats, Scott, and Emily and Charlotte Brontë. American writers associated with Romanticism included Longfellow, Poe, Emerson, Thoreau, Hawthorne, Melville, and Whitman.

There are two important reasons why the influence of Romanticism on the counterculture is not well known. First, despite its powerful impact on American culture, the counterculture is often dismissed as an ephemeral example of popular culture that is unworthy of serious attention from journalists and academics. Second, those who study the counterculture, Romanticism, modernism, and other sweeping movements in cultural history are extremely reluctant to generalize about these complex and often seemingly contradictory clusters of ideas.

In the preface to his book *The Making of a Counter Culture: Reflections on the Technocratic Society and Its Youthful Opposition*, Theodore Roszak notes that, "I have colleagues in the academy who have come within an ace of convincing me that no such things as 'The Romantic Movement' or 'The Renaissance' ever existed—not if one gets down to scrutinizing the microscopic phenomena of history."[4] Roszak proceeds to describe the counterculture's roots with countless examples from the Romantic Movement, but no general description of what the underlying philosophy of Romanticism might be.

It is critically important that people take the counterculture, its antecedents, and its successors seriously. It is vital that these broad movements in cultural history are made understandable to the general public. As difficult as this may be, the work of Isaiah Berlin has shown that it is not impossible. In his 1965 A. W. Mellon Lectures, which were published in 1999 under the title *The Roots of Romanticism*, Berlin argues against those who discourage the search for a definition of Romanticism. He explains that, "There *was* a romantic movement; it did have something which was central to it; it did create a great revolution in consciousness; and it is important to discover what this is."[5] With assistance from quotations from Isaiah Berlin, E. D. Hirsch Jr., Martha Bayles, and Robert Pattison, this section will describe the ideas of Romanticism and how these ideas have affected the counterculture and today's culture war debate.

Romanticism and Knowledge

Romanticism was a reaction against the extreme rationalism of the eighteenth-century Enlightenment. As Isaiah Berlin explains, "The Enlightenment supposed that there was a closed, perfect pattern of life. . . . There was some particular form of life and of art, and of feeling and of thought, which was correct, which was right, which was true and objective and could be taught to people if only we knew enough."[6] The Romantics rebelled against this ordered approach to knowledge and life, which they found to be stifling and woefully incomplete in its understanding. Berlin explains that the Romantics believed in:

> will, the fact that there is no structure to things, that you can mould things as you will—they come into being only as a result of your moulding activity—and therefore opposition to any view which tried to represent reality as having some kind of form which could be studied, written down, learnt, communicated to others, and in other respects treated in a scientific manner.[7]

Berlin explains that the various behaviors resulting from Romanticism were designed to challenge the Enlightenment order.

> In the eighteenth century you have an extreme order of sophistication . . . . Anything which destroys this, anything which blows it up, is welcome. Therefore whether you go to the Isles of the Blest, whether you go to the noble Indians, whether you go to the simple uncorrupted heart of the simple man, as sung of by Rousseau, on the one hand; or whether on the other hand you go to green wigs and blue waistcoats and men of wild distempers and people of the most extreme sophistication and savage bohemianism of life; whichever of these you go to, at any rate both are methods of blowing up, of shattering, that which is given.[8]

The Romantics' disbelief in the ability of people to develop a commonly shared knowledge of the world and the human condition was not only a break with the Enlightenment, but with the entire tradition of Western thought. Berlin describes Romanticism as "the largest recent movement to transform the lives and the thought of the Western world."[9] Robert Pattison describes Romanticism as "the Big Bang of

modern culture."[10] It is hard to overestimate the impact of this new way
of thinking. Romanticism sought not simply to break rules, but to do
away with rules altogether.

Romanticism and the Individual's Relationship to Society

Romanticism offered great support for the individual and individual
rights while showing great hostility toward society and its efforts to
provide education and shared social values. In his book *The Triumph of
Vulgarity: Rock Music in the Mirror of Romanticism*, Robert Pattison
summarizes Rousseau's *Social Contract* in the following manner.

> In Rousseau's theory, a man is free when he develops according to the
> dictates of nature. If he can avoid polluting contacts with civilization, he
> will grow up with his authenticity in tact. Civilization is corrupt because
> it takes natural men who are at one with nature and makes them smaller,
> turning citizens of the universe into mere Frenchmen, for instance, or re-
> ducing cosmic wisdom to the cliches of party platforms. All social asso-
> ciations are bad because they diminish the human wholeness of their
> members. In a perfect society, says Rousseau, men will avoid all associa-
> tions and retain their primitive virtue. If men in this primitive condition
> were ever called on to vote, they would share the same perspective on the
> issues because all would vote from the pure center of an identical integ-
> rity. They might not vote alike, but the coincidence of their perspective
> would guarantee that the result would be the dictate of what Rousseau
> calls "the general will." Make each self free and all selves will coincide.[11]

Romanticism had the beneficial effect of showing the limits of rationalism and the imperfections of society. This movement made powerful contributions to cultural life by promoting the importance of individual rights and the value of subjective experience. Romanticism,
however, suffered from its own set of serious limitations. Berlin describes these limitations as resulting from a failure to see the difference
between life and art.

> But their attempt to convert life into art presupposes that human beings
> are stuff, that they are simply a kind of material, even as paints or sounds
> are kinds of material: and to the degree to which this is not true, to the
> degree to which human beings, in order to communicate with each other,
> are forced to recognize certain common values, certain common facts, to
> live in a common world; to the extent to which not everything which sci-
> ence says is nonsense, not everything which common sense declares is
> untrue . . . to this extent romanticism in its full form, and even its off-

shoots in the form of both existentialism and Fascism, seems to me to be fallacious.[12]

Romanticism made a brilliant contribution to Western culture, but carried with it antisocial, antieducational values that have damaged individuals and society as a whole.

Despite the Romantic belief in the peaceful "natural" society, which was thought to exist at other times in history or among primitive cultures, Romanticism is deeply committed to conflict. As there is no structure to the universe other than that imposed by the individual will, it is understood that conflicts of will are bound to occur. Such conflicts are often resolved in violent clashes in which the stronger will prevails. In describing plays of the Romantic *Sturm und Drang (Storm and Stress)* movement of the late eighteenth century, Isaiah Berlin explains that at the core of this influential submovement within Romanticism is a "violent doctrine of personal self-assertion."[13]

Education from the Perspectives of Romanticism, the Enlightenment, and Puritanism

The combination of the belief that the world is unknowable and the belief that individual liberty should not be limited by society resulted in a very negative view of education. E. D. Hirsch Jr. explains the impact on education of two important ideas introduced by Romanticism.

> First, Romanticism believed that human nature is innately good, and should therefore be encouraged to take its natural course, unspoiled by the artificial impositions of social prejudice and convention. Second, Romanticism concluded that the child is neither a scaled-down adult nor a formless piece of clay in need of molding, rather, the child is a special being in its own right with unique, trustworthy—indeed holy—impulses that should be allowed to develop and run their course.[14]

This extremely positive view of human nature sees the individual as good and society's constraints upon the individual as evil. Traditional personal morality is viewed as a deadening social convention. Rationality and discipline in education are not favored because they tend to temper natural impulses.

Romanticism is, not surprisingly, strikingly different from the Enlightenment in its understanding of education. The Enlightenment position, which was dominant among our nation's Founding Fathers, took a more balanced view of human nature and a more positive view of society's role as educator. Enlightenment figures such as Thomas Jefferson were optimistic about human nature, but believed that individuals and society as a whole can succeed only if society educates individuals to avoid the pitfalls of human nature. Hirsch describes these reservations about human nature in the following passage.

> Although the thinkers of the Enlightenment broke with sectarian religion and the idea of original sin, most of them did not break with the molding and civilizing principles of education that had animated societies through history. The founders of the United States—Enlightenment figures like Madison and Jefferson . . . —took a skeptical and suspicious view of human nature.[15]

Hirsch explains that this skepticism is reflected in the checks and balances in the Constitution, which are essentially safeguards against the weaknesses of human nature.[16] James Madison summarized this view of the world in 1822 in the following way. "Popular government, without popular information, or the means of acquiring it, is but a prologue to a farce or a tragedy, or perhaps both. Knowledge will forever govern ignorance and a people who mean to be their own governors must arm themselves with the power which knowledge gives."[17]

Education in the Enlightenment understanding is society's support for the individual's free and purposeful pursuit of truth, a process that benefits both society and the individual. Both Puritanism and Romanticism tend to view education as coercive social indoctrination. The Puritan position, with its very dark view of human nature, affirms indoctrination and social control in general as long as it is based upon Puritan values. In his book *The Public Library in the Political Process*, Oliver Garceau describes Puritan education in seventeenth-century New England. "This educational system and its belief in individual learning were not democratic in the sense of assuming all men equal and free to rise by their own intellectual effort. Education and reading were to fit the citizen for his proper role in the theocratic state."[18] The Romantic position is critical of social indoctrination and demands that the individual be free to develop entirely personal intellectual pursuits.

Kay S. Hymowitz discusses the historical development of American education in her book *Ready or Not: Why Treating Children As Small Adults Endangers Their Future—and Ours*. Hymowitz describes our contemporary efforts to educate children as dominated by the "anticultural myth," which she describes as the assertion that "children are naturally moral creatures who are ruined by the adults who attempt to civilize them."[19] This myth, Rousseau's view of education, is the position of Romanticism. She notes that anticulturalism replaced an Enlightenment view of childhood and education that she describes as "republican," a view that had earlier replaced the authoritarian approach of Puritanism.

> By the early 1800s, ministers, intellectuals, and other cultural representatives began the process of framing what I'll be calling a "republican childhood," one in keeping with the ideals of the new country. Republican childhood had one central purpose: to vigorously prepare the young for freedom. In order to shape "self-governing" individuals, its architects rejected what until that time was an almost universal acceptance of corporal punishment and urged parents to appeal to their children's hearts and powers of reason. They encouraged them to awaken their children's minds and stir their interests by giving them time to play freely and by supplying the now recognizably middle-class home with toys and books. Yet republican childhood was still a serious business. Parents had to teach their children to balance personal ambition with a concern for the public good, respect for the law with critical independence, fidelity with entrepreneurial drive. No one believed that the transmission of these complex and highly contradictory cultural values would come naturally. Republican theorists saw it as a mammoth human undertaking, the psychic equivalent of digging a huge, multi-leveled, interconnected subway system. They believed that successful completion of this project required fifteen or twenty years, the hour-by-hour attentions of a mother, the emotional and financial support of a father, and the respectful attention of an entire society.[20]

These republican ideas led directly to the development of the institutions of public education.

Whereas the Enlightenment or republican approach views education as the pursuit of truth necessary to support complex decision making, education is viewed very differently under the Puritan or Romantic understanding. Education in either the Puritan or the Romantic view is not a moral struggle between good and evil or an intellectual struggle between truth and falsehood. Puritanism simply tells the individual what to believe and think. Romanticism regards tensions between good and evil or truth and falsehood to be irrelevant and misguided preoccupations of traditional culture. By stressing the innate goodness of human nature, the Romantics devalued the intellectual pursuit of truth as well as rational decision making. If everything is bound to end well naturally, why bother to work at goodness? Moral or intellectual struggle is not only not required to lead a good life; it is likely to be dangerously counterproductive.

Morality from the Perspectives of Romanticism, the Enlightenment, and Puritanism

It is at the point of discussing the moral implications of knowledge that the three-way debate becomes particularly intense. Both traditional Christianity and the secular philosophers of the Enlightenment accept what Isaiah Berlin calls "the old proposition that virtue is knowledge."[21] The truth about the world can be known and conforming to this truth will result in virtue and happiness. Christian and Enlightenment thinkers agreed that society must provide strong support by guiding individuals toward knowledge and by encouraging virtuous behavior.

To the Romantics, knowledge is not the source of virtue, but a source of self-deception and a tool for social control of the individual. The Romantic rejection of the validity of knowledge attained through tradition, reason, or any other method that can be shared by a society is deeply challenging to both Christianity and America's democratic form of government, which is based upon the rationality of the Enlightenment. The Romantic position is a profound denial of both the usefulness of shared knowledge and the authority of society to guide the individual toward conforming to this knowledge. The Romantic position authorizes and, to some extent, encourages individuals to ignore social mores whether derived from Christian tradition or from secular laws derived from reason. For both committed Christians and those who are committed to democracy, the proposal that moral values and public laws do not have authority and may be violated at will is a challenge of the most basic and extreme sort.

Romanticism and the Counterculture

The connection between Romanticism and the counterculture may be obvious from the foregoing discussion. This section will directly demonstrate this relationship.

In her book *Hole in Our Soul: The Loss of Beauty & Meaning in American Popular Music*, Martha Bayles explains how the ideas associated with Romanticism have continued to influence our culture in the traditions of modernism and postmodernism. Bayles describes Romanticism and its cultural successors as reacting against the narrow rationalism of the modern era.

This combination of credulity toward natural science and skepticism toward all other truth claims is central to the condition known as *modernity*. Some people date modernity to the Renaissance, others to the Enlightenment, and still others to the Industrial Revolution. However bounded, modernity should not be confused with modernism. On the contrary, modernism is best understood as a reaction *against* modernity. Or, to put it more accurately, modernism is the successor to the original reaction against modernity, which was romanticism.[22]

It is not possible here to detail the many important social and cultural movements that owe their perspective to the impulse of modernism that began with Romanticism. The important fact is that the counterculture took these ideas, which had for over one hundred and fifty years been on the fringe of the culture, to the center of the cultural stage. Ideas that were viewed as damaging but weak in influence were now popular enough to be a real threat to society.

As Bayles notes, the size and influence of the counterculture was frightening even to intellectuals sympathetic to modernism.

> The difference between the new radicalism of the late 1950s and the counterculture of the 1960s was, needless to say, one of scale. What began as the preoccupation of a tiny elite became the property of the public at large, with a speed that astonished all but the most prescient observers. The most prescient of these was Lionel Trilling, the literary dean of the New York intellectuals . . . . Having coined the phrase "adversary culture" to describe the generally hostile stance of modernism toward the rest of society, he began to express misgivings about the role played by educators like himself in transforming the anti-establishment literature of their youth into the established university curriculum.
>
> The older New York intellectuals were troubled by the nihilistic agenda of the beats. But it was Trilling who suggested, in a 1961 essay called "On the Teaching of Modern Literature," that his own career might have contributed to "the socialization of the anti-social, or the acculturation of the anti-cultural, or the legitimation of the subversive." He had good reason, since one of his most influential former students was Ginsberg. . . .
>
> Trilling took a gloomy view of what he called "modernism in the streets," assuming that modernism could not be popularized without being debased.[23]

To further demonstrate the connection between the counterculture and Romanticism, a discussion of the philosophy behind rock music is useful. This is the subject of both Martha Bayles's book and *The Triumph of Vulgarity: Rock Music in the Mirror of Romanticism* by Robert Pattison. Rock music was by far the most powerful medium used to communicate the values of the counterculture and an important reason why these values developed such pervasive influence in American life. Despite the negative sound of the titles of these books, both Bayles and Pattison have a strong appreciation for American popular music.

Robert Pattison describes the philosophy of Romanticism as *pantheism*. The pantheist perspective, he notes, is guided by instinct or feeling rather than reason. "When the pantheist equates self and God, he demotes thought to a secondary role in the universe and elevates feeling as the fundamental way of knowing." To illustrate this as a "central tenet of rock mythology," he quotes lyrics from the Troggs 1967 song "Love Is All Around Us." "My mind's made up by the way that I feel."[24]

Pattison finds that, like Romanticism, rock music is strongly opposed to society's traditional role as educator.

> Rock takes part in the Romantic anarchism which envisions a universe where wisdom is synonymous with energy, and so rock hates the inertia of stupidity as much as any rationalist. But in rock as in Rousseau, energy and wisdom are not fostered by formal education but by its abolition. "School's out forever," exults Alice Cooper. In rock mythology, schools mutilate instinct, killing energy and reason together.[25]

Pattison's description of Romanticism and the philosophy of rock music as pantheism provides a deeper view of the Romantics' positive view of human nature and the profound impact this view has on their approach to morality.

> There is no evil in the pantheist democracy because the transcendent vantage to distinguish good and evil has been gobbled up in the whole. Every act, no matter how loathsome by traditional standards, is valid, since the one knows itself by assuming the infinite forms of the many. To understand this process is to live "beyond the difference" between good and evil, refinement and vulgarity.[26]

The Romantics and their successors in rock music have, of course, had a long history of demonstrating "loathsome" acts. Such acts are performed for the dual purpose of demonstrating their philosophy and dismantling the dominant social order. Pattison connects this attitude in rock music to the Romantic tradition.

> Rock's hostility toward social order is another Romantic legacy. William Godwin, one of Rousseau's English disciples and Shelly's father-in-law, reduced his social philosophy to a Romantic epigram: "Everything that is

usually understood by the term cooperation, is, in some degree, an evil." .
. . Cooperation . . . is always self-limitation."[27]

As Pattison explains, the social hostility of contemporary forms of Romanticism, such as rock music, is often manifest in a combination of antisocial art combined with an apathetic disengagement from social life. "The rocker's apathy translates into decreasing percentages of voter participation and detachment from public debate and gainful employment."[28]

The part of Romanticism that reveled in the destruction of the prevailing culture lives on in a strain of modernism that Bayles refers to as "perverse modernism." Bayles quotes Lionel Trilling's description of the goal of this type of modernism as being "a negative transcendence of the human." She notes of perverse modernism that, "At its core it is anarchistic, hell-bent on disrupting the systematizing power of all organization, social as well as political."[29] Bayles finds that modernist perversity in rock music was clearly evident in the 1960s in the work of counterculture performers such as the Rolling Stones.[30] She reserves her greatest criticism, however, for successors in rap, punk, and alternative music who have taken this tradition to new depths. She explains that the "central argument" of her book is "that the anarchistic, nihilistic impulses of perverse modernism have been grafted onto popular music, where they have not only undermined the Afro-American tradition, but also encouraged today's cult of obscenity, brutality, and sonic abuse."[31]

Rock music and the counterculture share the Romantic philosophy of placing feeling above reason, its belief in the primacy of individual freedom, its general antagonism toward society, its special hatred for formal education, its commitment to conflict over cooperation or compromise, its rejection of traditional morality and civic duty, and its delight in watching mainstream society's horrified reaction to immoral behavior and art.

Libertarianism and the Antisocial Consensus of the 1980s

Robert Putnam describes the perspective of post-counterculture baby boomers as being "libertarian" in his book *Bowling Alone: The Collapse and Revival of American Community.* He explains that baby boomers have:

expressed more libertarian attitudes than their elders and less respect for
authority, religion, and patriotism. Comparisons of the high school
graduating classes of 1967 and 1973 make clear that even in high school
late boomers were less trusting, less participatory, more cynical about
authorities, more self-centered, and more materialistic, even by compari-
son to early boomers. Boomers in general are highly individualistic, more
comfortable on their own than on a team, more comfortable with values
than with rules.[32]

The lack of social participation that Putnam documents among baby
boomers is, in part, the result of the collapse of the revolutionary anarchism of the counterculture and the New Left. In her book *Connective
Leadership: Managing in a Changing World*, Jean Lipman-Blumen
explains that the collapse of counterculture politics was the result of too
little authority and structure.

In that heady era, "leadership" became the forbidden *L*-word. Many
groups deliberately prohibited official leaders; others featured rotating
leadership. Paradoxically, the revolt against hierarchy and elite leadership
structures led to what one political scientist labeled the "tyranny of
structurelessness."
     Ultimately, the structurelessness that enthralled the generation of the
sixties would prove to be a fatal organizational weakness. Eventually, the
structural vacuum simply bred exasperation, without building new and
enduring organizations or spawning the next generation of leaders. Indeed, many of these formless groups fragmented beyond repair.[33]

Although the social idealism of the counterculture faded, its belief in
individualism and its hostility toward social organization continued to
influence American politics in profound ways. E. J. Dionne Jr. explains
that the extreme antigovernment sentiment of the Reagan years of the
1980s was, in part, a contribution of the New Left.

Far from being inconsistent with the antiauthoritarian thrust of the 1960s,
much of what passed for conservative politics in the 1980s was really *libertarian*. Many young voters who had been drawn to the New Left and
the counterculture because they attacked authority were drawn to conservatism because it attacked the state. Thus did the New Left wage war
against the paternalistic liberal state and defeat it. The right picked up the
pieces.[34]

Francis Fukuyama describes the post-counterculture convergence of
the interests of the Left and Right as mutual support of:

a very powerful cultural theme: that of the liberation of the individual from unnecessary and stifling social constraints. . . .

Both the Left and Right participated in this effort to free the individual from restrictive rules, but their points of emphasis tended to be different. To put it simply, the Left worried about lifestyles, and the Right worried about money. . . .

As people soon discovered, there were serious problems with a culture of unbridled individualism, where the breaking of rules becomes, in a sense, the only remaining rule.[35]

The libertarian position is one of extreme individualism in both the social and economic areas of life. As libertarian scholar David Boaz explains the position:

On the contemporary American left-right spectrum, libertarianism is neither left nor right. Libertarians believe in individual freedom and limited government consistently, unlike either contemporary liberals or contemporary conservatives. Some journalists say that libertarians are conservative on economic issues and liberal on social issues, but it would make more sense to say that contemporary liberals are libertarian on (some) social issues but statist on economic issues, whereas contemporary conservatives are libertarian on (some) economic issues but statist on social issues.[36]

The Reagan era consensus was libertarian in that it gave the Left the social freedom it wanted and the Right the economic freedom it wanted. To forge this compromise, President Reagan presented the social conservatives of the Republican Party with moralistic rhetoric, but little real support for their issues.[37] In both the social and economic spheres, individualism triumphed over society's interest in curbing the excesses of individualism. Expressive individualism and utilitarian individualism joined forces to dominate American culture.

Utilitarian and Expressive Individualism in Historical Perspective

In *Habits of the Heart* Robert Bellah and his co-authors write, "By the end of the eighteenth century, there would be those who would argue that in a society where each vigorously pursued his own interest, the social good would automatically emerge. That would be utilitarian individualism in pure form."[38] Expressive individualism, on the other hand, was not the economic individualism so popular on the political

Right, but the direct contribution of Romanticism on the Left. Bellah and his associates demonstrate the relationship of these two types of individualism.

> By the middle of the nineteenth century, utilitarian individualism had become so dominant in America that it set off a number of reactions. A life devoted to the calculating pursuit of one's own material interest came to seem problematic for many Americans, some of them women, some of them clergymen, and some of them poets and writers. The cramped self-control of Franklin's "virtues" seemed to leave too little room for love, human feeling, and a deeper expression of the self. The great writers of what F. O. Matthiessen has called the "American Renaissance" all reacted in one way or another against this older form of individualism. In 1855 Hermann Melville published *Israel Potter*, a novel that subjected Franklin himself to bitter satire. Emerson, Thoreau, and Hawthorne put aside the search for wealth in favor of a deeper cultivation of the self. But it is perhaps Walt Whitman who represents what we may call "expressive individualism" in clearest form.[39]

The writers cited here are among the leading exponents of the Romantic movement in nineteenth-century America that includes the subtradition of transcendentalism.

What happened in the 1980s was an often-unconscious alliance between those interested in utilitarian individualism and in expressive individualism. The dominance of this governing coalition of interests resulted in greatly diminished influence for both the biblical tradition of America's dominant religions and the republican tradition of liberal democracy. Both of these traditions made important personal and public demands upon individuals that many now felt free to ignore.

Libertarian Individualism and Education

The libertarian consensus reduced education to the utilitarian pursuit of personal wealth and the equally individualistic pursuit of self-expression. As the social framework for education diminished, the idea of using one's talents for a social purpose declined. So much latitude was offered individuals in expressing themselves that the traditional project of using knowledge to make important personal and social judgments gave way to an indifferent relativism.

Allan Bloom in his 1987 book *The Closing of the American Mind* explains that the quest for openness and tolerance in individual expression has succeeded in making irrelevant the pursuit of truth and knowledge.

Thus there are two kinds of openness, the openness of indifference—promoted with the twin purposes of humbling our intellectual pride and letting us be whatever we want to be, just as long as we don't want to be knowers—and the openness that invites us to the quest for knowledge and certitude, for which history and the various cultures provide a brilliant array of examples for examination. This second kind of openness encourages the desire that animates and makes interesting every serious student—"I want to know what is good for me, what will make me happy"—while the former stunts that desire.

Openness, as currently conceived, is a way of making surrender to whatever is most powerful, or worship of vulgar success, look principled.[40]

Although Bloom's critique tends to be of the expressive individualism of the Left, it shows the relationship between the emptiness of expressive individualism and the emptiness of the Right's utilitarian individualism. Once education has been transformed from the pursuit of truth to mere self-expression, it has lost its moral purpose. Whatever cultural values are dominant will enter such a vacuum. Without a moral framework to provide social context, education is reduced to a quest for personal advancement in the marketplace.

Francis Fukuyama describes the libertarian support for intellectual and moral relativism in the following manner.

We are taught, moreover, that in negotiating among these competing cultural claims, none can be judged to be better than another. . . . This is a lesson taught not just by proponents of multiculturalism on the Left, but by libertarian economists on the Right, who boil down all human behavior to the pursuit of irreducible individual "preferences."[41]

Libertarian Individualism and Morality

Romanticism, the source of expressive individualism, is hostile to any social formulation of morality, whether based upon religious tradition or a rational conception of civic responsibility. Romanticism's connection to terms such as "counterculture," "adversary culture," and "perverse modernism" reflects this antagonistic relationship to society. As Romanticism is opposed to any type of social morality, it offers only the moral claims of the individual against society. This position is often expressed in an *anti-morality* that is a mere reaction to the prevailing social morality. Utilitarian individualism, which is dedicated to unrestrained economic freedom, is, on the other hand, at best *amoral* in its perspective. Neither expressive nor utilitarian individualism is a likely source of support for moral guidelines that limit individual freedom. If, as individualists imagine, shared social values limiting individual freedom were not necessary, the absence of such values would not be a problem. The 1960s, 1970s, and 1980s, however, have proven that the decline in social morality has had a profoundly negative social impact.

The General Social Impact of Libertarian Individualism

The blending of utilitarian and expressive individualism during the 1980s contributed to the decade's well-earned reputation as an antisocial period of self-absorption and greed. In *The New Golden Rule: Community and Morality in a Democratic Society*, sociologist Amitai Etzioni describes this period.

> The rise of the counterculture in the 1960s was followed in the 1970s, and especially in the 1980s, by a strong endorsement of a different, instrumental brand of individualism. It provided a normative seal of approval to a focus on the self rather than on responsibilities to the community, and saw in self-interest the best base for social order and virtue. . . .
> If the hallmark of the 1950s was a strong sense of obligation, from 1960 to 1990 there was a rising sense of entitlement and a growing tendency to shirk social responsibilities. Americans felt that government should be curtailed and that they should pay less taxes, but at the same time they demanded more government services on numerous fronts.[42]

The sociological impact of the shift toward extreme individualism after 1965 is documented by Francis Fukuyama in his book *The Great Disruption: Human Nature and the Reconstitution of Social Order*. He uses the term "social capital," which he defines as "a set of informal values or norms shared among members of a group that permits cooperation among them."[43] He finds that, "Beginning in about 1965, a large number of indicators that can serve as negative measures of social capital all started moving upward rapidly at the same time. These fell into three broad categories: crime, family, and trust."[44]

Fukuyama writes that the violent crime rate in the United States rose from an annual rate of 200 per 100,000 people in the mid-1960s to approximately 750 per 100,000 people at the peak in approximately 1991-92.[45] Fukuyama also documents a sharp increase in divorce beginning in the mid-1960s.

Approximately half of all marriages contracted in the 1980s in the United States could be expected to end in divorce. The ratio of divorced to married persons has increased at an even more rapid rate, due also to a parallel decline in marriage rates. For the United States as a whole, this rate has increased over fourfold in the space of just thirty years.[46]

Fukuyama explains that, "Trust is a key by-product of the cooperative social norms that constitute social capital. . . . In 1958, 73 percent of Americans surveyed said they trusted the federal government to do what is right either 'most of the time' or 'just about always.' By 1994, this figure had fallen as low as 15 percent . . . ."[47]

Robert Putnam reports steep declines in a wide range of forms of civic engagement over the past three decades. Declines in civic engagement from 1972-75 to 1996-98 were noted in areas such as reading a newspaper everyday, weekly church attendance, signing petitions, attending public meetings, writing a congressman, working for a political party, and running for or holding public office. Percentage declines were steep for baby boomers and even steeper for younger adults.[48] Putnam notes that overall "voting is down by about a quarter, and interest in public affairs by about one-fifth, over the last two or three decades."[49]

The extent to which the values of libertarian individualism contributed to this social disintegration is unclear. It is clear, however, that post-counterculture libertarianism helped to validate these negative changes. It is also clear that the reversal of this process of social disintegration that is now beginning has been accompanied by changes in the public's social philosophy. These changes have been due, in part, to the efforts of the community movement.

The Community Movement's Response to the Libertarian Consensus in the 1990s

Amitai Etzioni and other community movement writers who describe themselves as *communitarians* have articulated a powerful response to the libertarian consensus. Like the libertarian position, the communitarian point of view does not fit easily into the traditional liberal-conservative spectrum of politics. Etzioni describes the communitarian position as follows:

communitarian thinking leapfrogs the old debate between left-wing and right-wing thinking and suggests a third social philosophy. The basic reason this rearrangement is required is that the old map centers around the role of the government versus that of the private sector, and the authority of the state versus that of the individual. The current axis is the relationship between the individual and the *community*, and between freedom and order.[50]

Unlike the libertarian position, Etzioni's communitarianism does not attempt to be a consistent proponent or opponent of either the individual or society, but proposes that the relationship between the individual and society be brought into balance. As social morality and individual liberty are both found to be necessary facets of American culture, neither the biblical and republican traditions of social morality nor the traditions of utilitarian and expressive individualism are rejected. The result is a powerful synthesis of these cultural strands that acknowledges the importance of each strand while rejecting the excesses of those who advocate one or two of these cultural traditions at the expense of the others.

For example, communitarians remind expressive individualists that shared moral values are essential to the survival of any society. Communitarians are highly critical of the tendency of expressive individualists to support banning religious expression from public life. They believe that the Romantic dream of cultural anarchism cannot work in government or education because it is deeply contradicted by human nature. Whereas communitarians are critical of the excesses of the counterculture that were derived from Romanticism, they are generally supportive of the political projects supported by the counterculture, such as the civil rights movement, the women's movement, and the environmental movement.

Social conservatives who appreciate the biblical tradition are reminded by communitarians that Americans live in a pluralistic democracy, not a theocracy, and that the expression of individuals and other groups must be honored. Although shared values of social morality are vital to any culture, it is critically important in a democracy that no one group should impose its will on other groups. Dialogue is required to develop a consensus concerning the values shared among the nation's subcultures.

The support of communitarians for various types of social and governmental reforms to improve the health of the democracy confirms the close communitarian affiliation with the republican tradition. The communitarians demonstrate more respect for religion as a source for social morality than might have been granted by some secular Enlightenment thinkers, however. They also are more supportive of both utilitarian and expressive individualism than are some earlier proponents of the republican tradition. Although communitarians find the current culture to be unbalanced toward individualism, they do not seek a return to the extreme social discipline of the 1950s. Communitarians remind contemporary liberals that government cannot solve problems without support from other groups within society, such as private businesses and the institutions of civil society. They also remind liberals that success in solving social problems will require the active involvement and responsibility of those individuals suffering from these problems.

The communitarian position values the entrepreneurial spirit of utilitarian individualism and acknowledges the importance of this spirit to the economic and social success of our nation. Communitarians remind those who seek only economic freedom, however, of the disastrous impact of utilitarian individualism when it is not controlled by the traditions of social morality. The savings and loan scandal and the Wall Street scandals of the 1980s are memorable recent examples of utilitarian individualism unbounded by social morality.

The communitarian position is a powerful one because it acknowledges the importance of each of America's major cultural strands and effectively rejects the promotion of one or more strands at the expense of the others. By offering some support for each strand of America's political culture, the communitarian position has the potential to serve as a basis for compromise. By offering a critique of the excesses of those who do not seek a balanced approach, the communitarian position offers a strategy for the resolution of differences.

The power of this position was demonstrated repeatedly during the 1990s, as it was the organizing principle of government for President Clinton throughout his two terms in office. Tony Blair used the communitarian philosophy to reform the Labour Party in England and, in doing so, joined Bill Clinton in pursuing a political "third way" transcending the polarization of Left and Right.[51] Al Gore, Bill Bradley, George W. Bush, and John McCain each used aspects of the communitarian position in their campaigns for the presidency in 2000. The communitarian position is dominant in the Democratic Party. The influence of President Bush and his communitarian advisors has begun to change the essentially libertarian stance of the Republican Party.[52] Although people continue to describe American political conflicts as battles between conservatives and liberals, the deeper view of this struggle shows that the contest is now between libertarians and communitarians.

The consensus of the 1980s was one in which the post-counterculture Left and the mainstream of the conservative Right agreed that individual liberty from social constraint was of primary importance. This new consensus drove two important groups to the margins, social conservatives of the biblical tradition who were interested in moral constraints and traditional liberals of the republican tradition who believed in active government and various types of economic constraints. The communitarian position is a response to the libertarian consensus of the 1980s. The community movement seeks to balance individualism with a renewed sense of social morality and civic duty. A detailed explanation of communitarian thinking will be offered in chapter 3.

Conclusion

The cultural civil war that began in the 1960s with the rise of the counterculture has historical origins that must be understood if America is to resolve this conflict. To begin this process of understanding, it is useful to describe American culture using the categories of Robert Bellah and his associates in the book *Habits of the Heart: Individualism and Commitment in American Life*. They list the major strands of American culture as being biblical, republican, and modern individualist, with the modern individualist strand composed of expressive individualism and utilitarian individualism. The biblical tradition is the moral perspective of America's dominant religions. The republican tradition is the civic tradition of American democracy that grew out of the philosophical ideas of the eighteenth-century Enlightenment. Utilitarian individualism represents the economic freedom of the individual under capitalism. Expressive individualism represents the freedom of individual expression.

The cultural civil war has been a reaction to the greatly increased popularity of the ideas of expressive individualism, which were promoted by the counterculture. Expressive individualism, which is rooted in the ideas of Romanticism, challenges the authority of knowledge derived from tradition, reason, or any other means that can be communicated to form a social order. Expressive individualism is opposed to promoting social morality through education, law enforcement, or any other types of social persuasion or pressure. Such activities are viewed as unnecessary and unacceptable limitations of individual freedom. The counterculture of the 1960s brought these ideas, which had been at the fringe of the culture, to center stage.

These ideas presented a challenge of the most basic and extreme sort to those committed to the moral values of the biblical tradition and to those committed to the legal and ethical structure of the democracy. Traditional Christians were the first to resist these ideas. The Religious Right is now a powerful force within the Republican Party. Those representing the republican tradition of liberal democracy have also challenged expressive individualism. This faction, referred to here as the community movement, developed a political philosophy known as communitarianism that had a dominant influence within the Democratic Party during the 1990s. The communitarian position was a direct response to the libertarian social consensus of the 1980s, which combined expressive and utilitarian individualism.

The following chapter will demonstrate how this protracted social conflict has changed the public library as a national institution. The philosophy of the traditional public library, which is deeply rooted in the republican tradition, will be compared with the dominant ideology of the contemporary public library, which will be described as libertarian.

Notes

1. E. J. Dionne Jr., *Why Americans Hate Politics* (New York: Simon & Schuster, 1991), 11.

2. David S. Broder and Richard Morin, "Struggle over New Standards: Impeachment Reveals Nation's Changing Standards," *Washington Post*, 27 December 1998, 1(A).

3. Robert N. Bellah et al., *Habits of the Heart: Individualism and Commitment in American Life* (Berkeley: University of California Press, 1996), 27-28.

4. Theodore Roszak, *The Making of a Counter Culture: Reflections on the Technocratic Society and Its Youthful Opposition* (Garden City, N.Y.: Doubleday, 1969), xi.

5. Isaiah Berlin, *The Roots of Romanticism* (Princeton: Princeton University Press, 1999), 20.

6. Berlin, *Roots of Romanticism*, 105.

7. Berlin, *Roots of Romanticism*, 127.

8. Berlin, *Roots of Romanticism*, 135.

9. Berlin, *Roots of Romanticism*, 1.

10. Robert Pattison, *The Triumph of Vulgarity: Rock Music in the Mirror of Romanticism* (New York: Oxford, 1987), 108.

11. Pattison, *Triumph of Vulgarity*, 141-42.

12. Berlin, *Roots of Romanticism*, 145-46.

13. Berlin, *Roots of Romanticism,* 56.

14. E. D. Hirsch Jr., *The Schools We Need; And Why We Don't Have Them* (New York: Doubleday, 1996), 74.

15. Hirsch, *Schools We Need*, 75.

16. Hirsch, *Schools We Need*, 73.

17. Saul K. Padover, ed., *The Complete Madison: His Basic Writings* (New York: Harper, 1953), 337.

18. Oliver Garceau et al., *The Public Library in the Political Process* (Boston: Gregg Press, 1972), 5.

19. Kay S. Hymowitz, *Ready or Not: Why Treating Children As Small Adults Endangers Their Future—and Ours* (New York: Free Press, 1999), 6.

20. Hymowitz, *Ready or Not*, 10-11.

21. Berlin, *The Roots of Romanticism*, 118.

22. Martha Bayles, *Hole in Our Soul: The Loss of Beauty and Meaning in American Popular Music* (Chicago: University of Chicago Press, 1994), 34.

23. Bayles, *Hole in Our Soul*, 206-7.

24. Pattison, *Triumph of Vulgarity*, 89, 88.

25. Pattison, *Triumph of Vulgarity*, 104.

26. Pattison, *Triumph of Vulgarity*, 26-27.

27. Pattison, *Triumph of Vulgarity*, 142-43.

28. Pattison, *Triumph of Vulgarity*, 160.

29. Bayles, *Hole in Our Soul*, 45-46.

30. Bayles, *Hole in Our Soul*, 251.

31. Bayles, *Hole in Our Soul*, 12.

32. Robert D. Putnam, *Bowling Alone: The Collapse and Revival of American Community* (New York: Simon & Schuster, 2000), 258.

33. Jean Lipman-Blumen, *Connective Leadership: Managing in a Changing World* (Oxford: Oxford University Press, 1996), 65.

34. Dionne, *Why Americans,* 54.

35. Francis Fukuyama, *The Great Disruption: Human Nature and the Reconstitution of Social Order* (New York: Free Press, 1999), 13-14.

36. David Boaz, *Libertarianism: A Primer* (New York: Free Press, 1997), 21-22.

37. Dionne, *Why Americans*, 289-90.

38. Bellah, *Habits of the Heart*, 33.

39. Bellah, *Habits of the Heart*, 33.

40. Allan Bloom, *The Closing of the American Mind* (New York: Simon & Schuster, 1987), 41.

41. Fukuyama, *Great Disruption*, 16.

42. Amitai Etzioni, *The New Golden Rule: Community and Morality in a Democratic Society* (New York: Basic Books, 1996), 65.

43. Fukuyama, *Great Disruption*, 16.

44. Fukuyama, *Great Disruption*, 27.

45. Fukuyama, *Great Disruption*, 32.

46. Fukuyama, *Great Disruption*, 41.

47. Fukuyama, *Great Disruption*, 49.

48. Putnam, *Bowling Alone,* 252.

49. Putnam, *Bowling Alone,* 37.

50. Etzioni, *New Golden Rule,* 7.

51. Martin Walker, "Profile: Community Spirit Amitai Etzioni, Guru of the Clinton White House and One of the Most Controversial Thinkers in America, Brings His Message To Britain Today. His Speech Could Signpost a Future Labour Government's Social Policy," *The Guardian,* 13 March 1995.

52. Dana Milbank, "Needed: Catchword For Bush Ideology; 'Communitarianism' Finds Favor," *Washington Post,* 1 February 2001, final edition, sec. A, p. 1.

2

The Libertarian Public Library

Public librarians and trustees understand that antigovernment attitudes and the general decline in respect for social authority have hurt efforts to develop public libraries. Public librarians and trustees are, however, largely unaware of the ways in which the ideas of expressive and utilitarian individualism have contributed to this antisocial atmosphere and how these ideas have structured the response of library leaders to this environment. This is true, in part, because these ideas have been so absorbed into the conventional views of the majority that they are no longer clearly visible.

To demonstrate the influence of these ideas, it is necessary to analyze the ideology of the contemporary public library in the context of the history of the American public library. This chapter contrasts the traditional public library as envisioned by the founders of the Boston Public Library with the ideology of the contemporary public library, which reflects the libertarian social milieu of the 1980s. The 1852 report of the trustees of the Boston Public Library requesting tax support for the nation's first major public library will be used to describe the traditional public library. The Public Library Association's 1980 planning manual *A Planning Process for Public Libraries* and its successors will be used to describe the ideology of the libertarian public library. The report of the Boston trustees and the planning process manuals are important and influential documents that demonstrate the differences between a public library based upon the republican tradition of the Enlightenment and one based upon a libertarian philosophy derived from utilitarian individualism and the expressive individualism of Romanticism. The most basic change from the traditional public library to the libertarian public library is a change in mission from *education for a democratic society* to *access to information for individuals*.

It should be noted that, although the ideology of the public library is now predominantly libertarian, the institution itself is a blend of the traditional public library and its proposed replacement. The question of whether or not to complete the transition to the libertarian public library may be the most important question facing public librarians and trustees in the new century.

The Traditional Public Library

Boston Public Library, 1852

The modern public library movement began in Boston in 1852 when the trustees of the Boston Public Library submitted a report to the Boston City Council that requested tax support for a public library. This report is a clear and often profound rationale for the existence of the new institution. Any discussion of the mission of the modern public library must begin with this document.

The trustees of Boston argued that a public library was necessary to complete the city's system of public education. They wrote, "Although the school and even the college and the university are, as all thoughtful persons are well aware, but the first stages in education, the public makes no provision for carrying on the great work. . . . It awakens a taste for reading, but it furnishes to the public nothing to read."[1] They found the public library to be necessary because "ampler means and means better adapted to our peculiar needs and wants, are demanded, in order to diffuse through our society that knowledge without which we have no right to hope, that the condition of those who are to come after us will be as happy and prosperous as our own."[2]

The Boston trustees viewed this new institution as important both to the growth of individuals and to the political, economic, and social advancement of the community.

> And yet there can be no doubt that such reading ought to be furnished to all, as a matter of public policy and duty, on the same principle that we furnish free education, and in fact, as a part, and a most important part, of

the education of all. For it has been rightly judged that,—under political, social and religious institutions like ours,—it is of paramount importance that the means of general information should be so diffused that the largest possible number of persons should be induced to read and understand questions going down to the very foundations of social order, which are constantly presenting themselves, and which we, as a people, are constantly required to decide, and do decide, either ignorantly or wisely.[3]

The Boston trustees leave no doubt that this new institution is to be for all economic classes of people. "Above all, while the rightful claims of no class,—however highly educated already,—should be overlooked, the first regard should be shown, as in the case of our Free Schools, to the wants of those, who can, in no other way supply themselves with the interesting and healthy reading necessary for their farther education."[4] They explicitly mention the need for outreach to the poor, noting that they regard it "as a great matter" to carry as many books as possible "into poor families" and "into cheap boarding houses . . . to affect life and raise personal character and condition."[5]

The Boston trustees viewed the public library as an educational institution, "the crowning glory of our system of City schools."[6] This new institution was to help individuals grow through education and to serve as a "means of public improvement."[7] They were conscious, as the best exponents of American society have always been, that democratic institutions require an informed citizenry and that government officials and the public as a whole have a duty to support and encourage the education of the entire community.

The traditional public library as described by the Boston trustees clearly grows out of the Enlightenment philosophy that underlies our democratic form of government. In his essay "The Study of American Library History," Jesse Shera explains that, "The concept of the library as an educational agency is a direct transfer to librarianship of nineteenth century faith in the education of the masses, a faith that had its roots in the eighteenth-century Enlightenment and the belief in the idea of progress and the perfectibility of man."[8]

It is not surprising that George Ticknor, the primary author of the report of the Boston trustees, was a young friend of Enlightenment genius Thomas Jefferson. As Oliver Garceau wrote in his book *The Public Library in the Political Process*, "Through Ticknor we join hands with the eighteenth century. For ten years he had been a correspondent of Jefferson. He translated the passionate humanism of the eighteenth century into nineteenth-century terms."[9] Garceau quotes the following

passage from Jefferson's 1809 letter to John Wyche to show the simi-
larity between the ideas of Ticknor and Jefferson.

> The people of every country are the only safe guardians of their own
> rights, and are the only instruments which can be used for their destruc-
> tion. And certainly they would never consent to be so used were they not
> deceived. To avoid this they should be instructed to a certain degree. I
> have often thought that nothing would do more extensive good at small
> expense than the establishment of a small circulating library in every
> county, to consist of a few well-chosen books, to be lent to the people of
> the country under such regulations as would secure their safe return in
> due time. These should be such as would give them a general view of
> other history, and a particular view of that of their own country, a toler-
> able knowledge of geography, the elements of Nature, Philosophy, of Ag-
> riculture, and Mechanics.[10]

The Traditional Public Library since 1852

The traditional public library, which is committed to education for a
democratic society, has had an amazing history that can be no more
than referenced here. Patrick Williams tracks the institutional mission
of education for the advancement of society through the history of the
public library in his book *The American Public Library and the Problem of Purpose*. Williams discusses the important controversy concerning the educational value of popular fiction in the late nineteenth
century, the growth of the public library as a militantly educational
institution during the Progressive Era, the public library's active participation in the Adult Education Movement between 1920 and 1948,
and the aggressive social outreach efforts of the late 1960s and early
1970s.

A particularly interesting examination of the strengths and failings of
the traditional public library is found in the reports of the Public Library Inquiry, which were published in the late 1940s and early 1950s.
The Public Library Inquiry was a comprehensive study of the public
library written by an independent group of social scientists led by political scientist Robert D. Leigh. These reports offer an interesting and
sometimes brilliant outside assessment of public libraries and public
librarianship. Perhaps more important than the recommendations offered in these reports is the detailed view they offer of the public library
almost exactly one hundred years after the founding of Boston Public
Library.

Leigh and his associates found that public librarians still followed
their traditional purpose of providing education for our democratic so-

ciety. Interest in this traditional mission was no doubt heightened by the threat to democratic society posed by World War II. Librarians were still very much motivated by the traditional optimism concerning the perfectibility of man through education. The researchers referred to this belief in the "ameliorative quality" of books as the "Library Faith."[11] Public Library Inquiry researchers believed that the serious educational and civic purposes detailed in mid-century lists of national library objectives provided a reasonable basis for the mission of the public library. They cautioned, however, that only a minority of the population demonstrates an interest in serious education and intense involvement in civic life. As Douglas Raber notes in his book *Librarianship and Legitimacy: The Ideology of the Public Library Inquiry*, Robert Leigh and Oliver Garceau agreed that "the audience for public library services is necessarily small."[12]

To test the support for official objectives, the Public Library Inquiry researchers sent 110 librarians a consolidated list of objectives developed from three separate American Library Association documents produced in the 1940s. This list of objectives, which was supported by a strong majority of the librarians surveyed, is worthy of note because it strongly supports the social purposes of the institution. The consolidated list's "General Definition of Objectives" denotes the following as the first of three major objectives, "To assemble, preserve, and administer books and related educational materials in organized collections, in order to promote, through guidance and stimulation, an enlightened citizenship and enriched personal lives." The text supporting these objectives places a great stress on citizenship with references to "understanding the democratic processes of group life" as well as preserving "the precious heritage of freedom of expression." Providing "lectures, forums, and discussion groups" is recommended.[13] The section titled "Stimulation and leadership" includes the following passage.

> The library, in co-operation with all other agencies of education and information, should seek to increase the competence of people to form sound judgments and to realize that they should not only understand about important public problems, but also express their opinions and act in accordance with their judgment.
>
> The library should assist in the establishment and improvement of community group programs, and adapt programs to the interests of special groups. At the same time, the library's duty remains that of providing reliable information on all sides of controversial questions.[14]

Under "Emphasis" the list notes that libraries should "contribute directly to the solution of the crucial problems of our time."[15]

Throughout the years from 1852 through roughly 1972, librarians and trustees experienced a series of idealistic efforts to fulfill the public library's mission of education for a democratic society. These efforts were punctuated by periods of disillusionment and retreat in which librarians realized that their high expectations had not been met. Since the early 1970s, library leaders have retreated from the optimistic social mission of the traditional public library.

The Libertarian Public Library and *A Planning Process for Public Libraries*, 1980

In the wake of the cultural civil war of the 1960s, the public library's republican mission of education for a democratic society declined sharply under the challenge of a libertarian mission of access to information for individuals. The new public library, like the cultural consensus from which it is derived, was the product of the expressive individualism of the Left and the utilitarian individualism of the Right. The 1947 *A.L.A. National Plan*, cited by Oliver Garceau, describes the traditional public library as balanced between service to society and the individual. "The objectives of the public library are many and various. But in essence they are two—to promote enlightened citizenship and to enrich personal life. They have to do with the twin pillars of the American way, the democratic process of group life and the sanctity of the individual person."[16] The libertarian consensus of the 1980s sought to create a culture that acknowledged only the autonomy of the individual. Public library development changed to reflect this new approach.

Expressive Individualism and the Libertarian Public Library

E. J. Dionne Jr. noted that the New Left defeated "the paternalistic liberal state."[17] This can be viewed as a triumph of the expressive individualism of the Romantic tradition over the republican tradition of social morality. Expressive individualism's primary contribution to the cultural atmosphere of the 1980s was a reluctance to promote social goals or to exercise social authority in any way. A relativistic approach to knowledge and open hostility toward all figures of social authority deeply challenged educational authorities in public schools and in public libraries. Relativism proclaimed that all interpretations of reality were equally valid. In this climate, teachers and librarians were not needed to interpret the world and their interpretations were viewed as unwelcome social efforts to suppress the interpretations of individuals and interest groups. The new order called for the liberation of education from the social purposes of educational authorities.

The Revisionist Historians Challenge the Traditional Public Library

The influence of these ideas on public libraries was clearly visible in attempts in the 1970s by revisionist library historians such as Michael Harris and Dee Garrison to discredit the republican orientation of the leaders of the traditional public library. The new interpretation found, for example, that George Ticknor and the other original Boston Public Library trustees were committed not to democracy and education, but to elitism and social domination. Michael Harris argued that "American librarians have been generally convinced of the truth of a warm and comforting explanation of the origins, and consequent growth, of the American public library." He found that the public library movement did not stem from "a passion of liberal and humanitarian zeal," but from an effort to control rebellious Irish immigrants that was characterized by "authoritarianism and elitism."[18]

Dee Garrison in her book *Apostles of Culture: The Public Librarian and American Society, 1876-1920* also questions the "progressive interpretation" of the public library and its origins. Although Garrison claims to present a measured and balanced analysis, her work seeks to prove her thesis that "problems associated with sex and class played a dominant part in the formulation of the public library and the ideology of library leadership." Like Harris, Garrison questions the social authority and the motivations of those who sought to educate the public through the public library. She notes that "all institutions practice social control and that the upper-class orientation and administration of the public library should come as no surprise to anyone. It is the purpose of ruling elites, after all, to perpetuate their power by disseminating their own cultural values, and this is true even in political democracies."[19] This critique, of course, does not accept the possibility that an educated elite might have altruistic motives or that the sharing of the values of the elite might have a positive effect on society. Any such sharing is viewed as an oppressive and authoritarian means of indoctrination.

Garrison finds moral leadership to be particularly offensive. The derisive intention of the book's title is evident in the following passage describing the librarians of the period. "With a cultural arrogance lim-

ited only by their moral sincerity, they upheld their mission to serve the
masses who supposedly sought material and moral advancement
through education."[20] In the work of both Harris and Garrison, library
leaders are found to be at once pragmatic oppressors of the common
man and idealistic optimists about the prospect of educating the common man.

Behind this radical critique, which contributed to the libertarian
public library, is the Romantic belief that society does not have the
right to educate or socialize individuals in any way. In accord with the
values of expressive individualism, the libertarian public library takes
the side of individuals whenever there is a conflict between individual
rights and the needs of society or social entities. As noted earlier, the
Enlightenment perspective of the traditional public library is very different from the Romantic philosophy of the counterculture in regard to
social authority.

The dour assessment of the founders of the public library and their
successors that is presented by Harris and Garrison makes sense if
viewed through the lens of Romanticism. If human nature is innately
good, there is no need for education or leadership of any kind. People
need to be free from social controls to follow their natural instincts.
Those who attempt to shape the lives of others violate the individual
freedom of those whom they seek to teach or lead. The radically egali-
tarian approach to the public library that Harris and Garrison appear to
prefer would respond to individual needs, not social purposes such as
the support of the democracy. In this view, education and leadership
oppress individuals and are therefore morally reprehensible. To the
post-counterculture Left, any exercise of social authority is unacceptably coercive and authoritarian. No form of social authority can claim to
be valid and no form of knowledge can claim to be true. This position
is the opposite of the authoritarian position of the Puritans of the Religious Right. The false choices of the culture war are between anarchy
and authoritarianism in the life of society and between relativism and
absolutism in the intellectual life.

A Planning Process for Public Libraries and Expressive Individualism

The challenge of expressive individualism for librarians and trustees
was to lead without leading and educate without educating. Although
this has a certain mystical appeal, it is difficult to understand how such
a self-contradictory project can succeed on the plane of everyday exis-

tence. To approach this difficult task, library leaders relied on the still popular concept of the general will, which Romanticism obtained from Rousseau. The belief in the superiority of the general will of the community over the authority and leadership of librarians and trustees is evident throughout the 1980 publication *A Planning Process for Public Libraries*, the first of several planning manuals prepared for the Public Library Association.

The authors of *A Planning Process for Public Libraries* contended that, "It is not the library that is making decisions about what it will do for its community so much as the community which is deciding what it wants its library to be."[21] The strategy of developing libraries through the leadership of people like the Boston Public Library trustees of 1852 was to be replaced by a heightened sensitivity to the voice of the people. It was assumed that, if the will of the people were understood, the public library based upon this understanding would be an improved and more inclusive institution. In keeping with this approach, this manual carefully avoids prescribing social purposes and discourages the measurement of a community's library by any external standard.

After referencing the more traditional public library mission of meeting the "cultural, educational, informational, and recreational needs" of the community; the authors of *A Planning Process for Public Libraries* stated, "The ultimate purpose of any library is to meet the information needs of its community." Information was defined to include "all knowledge, ideas, facts, and imaginative works of the mind which have been communicated, recorded, published and/or distributed formally or informally in any format."[22] This striking shift from education to information demonstrated the desire among librarians to avoid the uncomfortable position of functioning as educators and leaders in an era hostile toward attempts to shape the behavior of sovereign individuals. A safer, more desirable role was seen to be to simply provide access to information, bits of content offered without the intention to persuade people what to think or how to understand.

In following the wisdom of the people and honoring individual liberty, the new institution no longer claimed to overtly educate the community, no longer claimed to prescribe specific social outcomes. Librarians and trustees, under the influence of the ideas of Romanticism, were no longer confident in their ability to understand the world; they no longer believed in their right to exercise the social authority of educators and community leaders. This led to a shift in the mission of the institution from education for a democratic society to the more utilitarian mission of providing access to information for individuals.

A Planning Process for Public Libraries leaned heavily toward demand in the traditional debate between quality and demand in materials
selection. In doing so, it followed the example of Charles Robinson
who led Baltimore County Public Library to popularize a demand-
oriented approach to public library development in the late 1970s. In
The Public Library and the Problem of Purpose, Patrick Williams
notes the repeated use of "most-wanted" in the manual's role statements. Williams explains that, "A planning document so friendly to
public demand seemed to be a planning document for a people's library."[23] The traditional concern for quality in materials selection was
eclipsed by the need to meet popular demand.

The concern for the welfare of the community that is found in many
general statements in the report of the trustees of Boston Public Library
appears to be lost somewhere in between the grandiose conjecture of
the 1979 publication *The Public Library Mission Statement and Its Imperatives for Service,* which the authors reference, and the fixation
upon service to individuals found in *A Planning Process for Public
Libraries.* After discussing a series of problems that could best be described as international, *The Public Library Mission Statement and Its
Imperatives for Service* offers a perplexingly broad definition of community. "*Community* means not only a narrow geographic service support area but also the wider area—to which every local library must be
connected."[24] From this idea of a community without boundaries, the
authors of *A Planning Process for Public Libraries* move to their own
concept of community, which appears to be a collection of individuals
rather than a social environment that is home to individuals.

> Communities don't have information needs; individuals do. Needs
> vary from one person to another and for the same person over time.
> However, by looking at the characteristics of the individuals within
> a community, such as their ages, levels of education, and occupa-
> tions, the library can predict to a certain extent the kinds of infor-
> mation that will be needed overall. Characteristics of the commu-
> nity itself, such as its location, the availability of educational and
> cultural facilities, and its major industries and businesses will also
> influence the kinds of information that its population may need.[25]

The sort of study advised here offers little encouragement to ascertain
or respond to specific problems that might exist for families, neighborhoods, churches, civic organizations, or the community as a whole.

A Summary of the Influence of Expressive Individualism on the Libertarian Public Library

The victory of the expressive individualism of the counterculture over the social morality of the republican tradition deeply undercut the republican project of public education. As the social perspective necessary to support the democracy declined in American culture, the authority of public schools and public libraries to define knowledge and educate citizens was challenged. Since the 1960s, American society's relativistic approach to knowledge and intense hostility toward social authorities have severely damaged public education in all of its forms.

Utilitarian Individualism and the Libertarian Public Library

Unlike the report of the Boston trustees, which makes moral claims upon the community and its leaders to provide education through the public library, *A Planning Process for Public Libraries* does not speak in moral terms. If the public library is not dedicated to a positive social goal such as education, no basis for such moral claims exists. The libertarian public library is viewed as utilitarian, an amoral function of the marketplace. Libraries will be supported if they are found to be useful. Usefulness is a function of effective planning that ensures responsiveness to the information needs of individuals.

The second part of E. J. Dionne Jr.'s quote about libertarianism should be remembered here. After noting that the New Left defeated the paternalistic liberal state, he explains that, "The right picked up the pieces."[26] The political Right, in the form of the utilitarian individualism of the marketplace, provides the developmental methodology of the libertarian public library. The values and strategies of the marketplace entered the vacuum resulting from the loss of the traditional mission of education for a democratic society.

The private sector's strategies of customer service improvement, marketing, and strategic planning increasingly replaced more traditional public library development strategies in the 1970s as librarians and trustees sought to reproduce the innovations of Baltimore County Public Library. Private sector developmental strategies gained powerful national influence with the publication of *A Planning Process for Public Libraries.* The new definition of information helped library leaders think of their service as the distribution of a commodity, rather than as a complex human interaction. The selection of library roles and service responses in the later editions of the planning manual made it increasingly clear that the planning process for public libraries is closely modeled after the private sector's development of market niches.

The generalist nature of the public library as an institution did not discourage the authors of these manuals from advocating ever-increasing specialization in the services offered. By concentrating resources and limiting market niches, a library will be able to provide excellent service and receive strong public support according to this line of reasoning. In a manner characteristic of the amorality of utilitarian individualism, these manuals approach the possible roles and service responses with the indifferent relativism of the marketplace.

The relativism of utilitarian individualism complements the relativism of expressive individualism, but it is very different. The purpose here is not unfettered expression, but the economic freedom to sell whatever you choose. The important question for utilitarian individualism is clearly not determining the nature of the service to be provided or the relationship of this service with the national institution. The important question is whether the service will be popular with a sufficient number of individuals to obtain financial support. As in the private sector, it does not matter what you sell as long as you can make a profit. Today private sector developmental strategies are so well accepted in public libraries that many librarians refer to their "customers" rather than their "patrons" or their "users." The term "marketing" is often used in place of "community relations" or "public relations."

Despite the fundamental differences between public- and private-sector organizations, public libraries like other public institutions are now being developed using techniques that assume that these differences do not exist. In this view, the libertarian public library is intended to function as a specialized, demand-based materials distribution service in the style of the private sector, but with a public subsidy.

Conclusion

The contemporary public library is a blend of the traditional public library and the libertarian public library. From the traditional public library to today's more libertarian public library, library leaders have moved from a position of asserting cultural leadership to one better described as following the general will of the public. They have moved from a mission of education to one that seeks to provide access to information. A stress on the social impact of the institution has been replaced by a dominant interest in satisfying individual users. They have moved from defending the institution in moral terms to defending the institution on the basis of its public use and popularity. This transition is, of course, not complete.

In deciding whether the transition to the libertarian public library should be continued, library leaders need to recognize that a social institution based on unbounded individualism is a very shaky edifice indeed. The expressive individualism of Romanticism fails to provide a strong foundation for education and social development because it does not believe in rational knowledge and it does not believe in society's authority to influence the behavior of the individual. The amorality of the marketplace contributed by utilitarian individualism is also an unlikely foundation for a social institution. Utilitarian individualism is traditionally indifferent to the welfare of society. The antisocial and morally empty underpinnings of the libertarian public library will become increasingly clear if the traditional public library is further subplanted by the libertarian model. In the long term, the degraded mission of access to information for individuals will not succeed in the political process. It will not win the moral and financial support of society.

The chapters that follow offer an alternative to the libertarian public library that builds upon the long history of the public library as an educational institution supporting social development. The alternative suggested here is not, however, simply a return to the past. It is clear that the traditional public library has been a mixture of success and failure. The alternative proposed here is based upon the traditional public library, but seeks to take that tradition several important steps forward with the help of new ideas from the community movement. After a more detailed description of community movement ideas, the remainder of this book will be dedicated to defining civic librarianship, demonstrating the impact of this new approach on public library service, and assessing the importance of civic librarianship to the future of the public library.

Notes

1. Jesse H. Shera, *Foundations of the Public Library: Origins of the Public Library Movement in New England 1629-1855* (Chicago: University of Chicago Press, 1949; n.p.: Shoe String Press, 1965), 272.

2. Shera, *Foundations*, 279.

3. Shera, *Foundations*, 281.

4. Shera, *Foundations,* 282.

5. Shera, *Foundations,* 286.

6. Shera, *Foundations,* 287.

7. Shera, *Foundations,* 288

8. Jesse H. Shera, "On the Value of Library History," in *Reader in American Library History,* ed. Michael H. Harris (Washington, D.C.: NCR Microcard Editions, 1971), 9.

9. Oliver Garceau et al., *The Public Library in the Political Process* (Boston: Gregg Press, 1972), 30-31.

10. Garceau, *Public Library,* 31.

11. Robert D. Leigh, *The Public Library in the United States* (New York: Columbia University Press, 1950), 14.

12. Douglas Raber, *Librarianship and Legitimacy: The Ideology of the Public Library Inquiry* (Westport, Conn.: Greenwood Press, 1997), 71.

13. Leigh, *Public Library,* 16-17.

14. Leigh, *Public Library,* 18-19.

15. Leigh, *Public Library,* 19.

16. Garceau, *Public Library,* 143-44

17. E. J. Dionne Jr., *Why Americans Hate Politics* (New York: Simon & Schuster, 1991), 54.

18. Michael Harris, "The Purpose of the American Public Library," *Library Journal* 98, no. 16 (15 September 1973): 2509, 2511.

19. Dee Garrison, *Apostles of Culture: The Public Librarian and American Society, 1876-1920* (New York: Free Press, 1979), xi, xii, xiii.

20. Garrison, *Apostles,* xiv.

21. Vernon E. Palmour, Marcia C. Bellassai, and Nancy V. De Wath, *A Planning Process for Public Libraries* (Chicago: American Library Association, 1980), 7.

22. Palmour, Bellassai, and De Wath, *Planning Process,* 9, 41, 41.

23. Patrick Williams, *The American Public Library and the Problem of Purpose* (New York: Greenwood Press, 1988), 123.

24. Public Library Association, *The Public Library Mission Statement and Its Imperatives for Service* (Chicago: American Library Association, 1979), 5.

25. Palmour, Bellassai, and De Wath, *Planning Process,* 8.

26. Dionne, *Why Americans,* 54.

3

The Community Movement

The perspective of the community movement was introduced in the discussion of America's cultural civil war. This chapter will present a more detailed description of community movement ideas and will analyze the importance of these ideas to American society. The remainder of the book will discuss how these ideas can be used to improve public libraries.

The community movement is a response to the libertarian consensus of the 1980s. The libertarian consensus promoted extreme social and economic individualism unbounded by the biblical and republican traditions of social morality. The social deterioration that resulted, in part, from this dominance of expressive and utilitarian individualism is well documented. This decline created a powerful demand for new ways to strengthen the nation's endangered social structures. This demand was met by a broad-based intellectual effort. Many contributors to this movement describe their ideas by using the term "communitarian."

Communitarian ideas have a clear relationship to the ideas of the republican tradition of the Enlightenment. The Founding Fathers were optimistic but skeptical about human nature, which they believed was a mixture of good and evil. They believed that society needed to help individuals to make personal and social choices between good and evil. Although laws were developed to prohibit certain choices, the primary means of helping individuals to make good choices was through the provision of education. An informed and productive citizenry fully engaged in the life of the community was viewed as the basic requirement for democracy. The Founding Fathers were committed to individual freedom within a context of deep concern for the individual's responsibility to help maintain a strong society through voting and all other forms of civic involvement.

Whereas the perspective of the community movement is similar to the philosophy of the Enlightenment in its view of human nature, education, and the individual's relationship with society, the community movement is much more than a restatement of the republican views of the Founding Fathers. Community movement writers bring a modern perspective, contemporary ideas, and a wide variety of intellectual disciplines to the discussion of this traditional perspective. The resulting perspective offers a deeper, more holistic understanding of America's entire cultural heritage and provides new strategies for fulfilling the dream of those who set the foundations for American society.

The moderate, centrist nature of the communitarian position is evident in the community movement's evaluation of the social reforms of the 1960s. Amitai Etzioni describes the communitarian position as supportive of much of the social reform of the 1960s. In the following passage, he expresses his concern, however, that new social constructs have often not been developed to replace those that were torn down. "Since the early sixties, many of our moral traditions, social values, and institutions have been challenged, often for valid reasons. The end result is that we live in a state of increasing moral confusion and social anarchy."[1] Although not a realistic goal, destroying the old order without replacing it with a new order was exactly what the counterculture intended. In taking this position, the counterculture was perfectly in tune with the tradition of Romanticism. As Isaiah Berlin noted of Romanticism, "Rules must be blown up as such."[2] This disbelief in social order continues to hamper the construction of a new social order.

Amitai Etzioni has described the community movement as an "environmental movement" to save America's endangered social environment.[3] Etzioni and fellow sociologists such as Robert Bellah have been at the forefront of this movement to strengthen social structures such as families, neighborhoods, churches, civic groups, and communities. They believe that the serious problems that confront these social structures have been caused, in part, by extreme individualism unbounded by social morality. They seek to restore moral order to American society. They have sought to transcend cultural warfare and political gridlock by developing a new framework for social and political dialogue. The culture war's choice of authoritarian moral coercion or the complete absence of a social code of morality is viewed as a false choice in the communitarian framework. The communitarian position finds the political choice between solving social problems through the government or through the private sector to be equally false.

Communitarians urge balancing the rights of individuals with their social responsibilities. They have called for a strong but inclusive social morality that is in striking contrast to both the moral silence of the civil libertarian Left and the moral exclusivity of the social conservatives of the Right. Communitarians rely heavily upon education and dialogue to develop moral consensus rather than abandoning the process of consensus building as the civil libertarian Left has done or advocating coercive enforcement of moral values in the manner of the social conservatives of the Right. The communitarian approach is not as reliant upon government solutions as the traditional Left due to a belief that solving social problems requires comprehensive community support as well as the responsibility of individuals to help themselves. The communitarian approach differs from the political Right in that it finds that government does have an important role to play in solving social problems. As noted in chapter 1, the communitarian position seeks to balance individual freedom and social order by seeking equilibrium among the republican and biblical traditions of social morality and the expressive and utilitarian traditions of individualism.

To further describe the communitarian perspective, this chapter will first discuss how the literature of the community movement can help Americans to see and understand the nation's endangered social environment. Next, this literature will be used to demonstrate the role of social authority in a democratic society and the importance of balancing rights and responsibilities. Community movement strategies for strengthening communities will then be presented. The chapter will conclude with a discussion of the general contributions of the community movement to American society.

Seeing Our Endangered Social Environment

The Challenge of a New Paradigm

The community movement represents a new paradigm for looking at knowledge and the relationship of the individual and society. Although the concept of *paradigm shifting* has been overused and trivialized, this concept is both appropriate and indispensable for the discussion of the change in perspective required to understand community movement ideas. Joel Barker describes paradigms in his book *Paradigms: The Business of Discovering the Future.* "A paradigm is a set of rules and regulations (written or unwritten) that does two things: (1) it establishes or defines boundaries; and (2) it tells you how to behave inside the boundaries in order to be successful."[4] Another way to describe a paradigm is as a "Thoughtworld," a concept used very effectively in E. D. Hirsch Jr.'s critique of the impact of Romanticism upon public education in his book *The Schools We Need and Why We Don't Have Them.*[5]

One of the interesting features of paradigms is that people become so accustomed to using them to make sense of the world that the view they provide gradually becomes indistinguishable from reality itself. It becomes difficult to see beyond the Thoughtworld. This is so much the case that most people using paradigms are utterly unconscious of the fact that they are using a lens to see the world.

In discussions of community movement ideas among both librarians and journalists, a common sentiment might be summarized in the following way. "I don't want to consider this philosophical position because having a philosophy would reduce my objectivity." The assumption here is that being unconscious of the filter through which a person sees reality is equivalent to having no filter at all. This, of course, ignores the fact that everyone has to use a philosophical paradigm to see the world. Existence is far too complex for anyone to approach it without some form of mediating cultural structure. The choice then is not between having a philosophy and not having one, but between alternative philosophies. People should choose among philosophies according to their ability to explain the world and provide a basis for appropriate action. The less conscious a person is of the philosophical paradigm she or he uses, the more likely they are to fail to be objective.

Examining a new paradigm is extremely challenging because seeing the world in a fundamentally new way may result in major changes in both a person's professional and personal life. Those who were in college in the late 1960s and early 1970s remember the revolutionary changes that resulted from the paradigm shift initiated by the counterculture and the New Left. The social landscape changed fundamentally. People were affected in everything from marriage to religion to career choices. People risk a great deal in changing basic paradigms and should resist such changes unless the new paradigm can offer a superior lens through which to observe the world. If the new paradigm is in fact a superior lens, the power to be gained from the clearer view of the world that it provides can be immense.

The paradigm shift described here as the community movement, although by nature less flamboyant than the counterculture, is potentially as powerful. This perspective has deeply influenced all four major candidates for the presidency in 2000 and may well be considered the dominant political perspective of the entire decade of the 1990s. This is not to say, however, that public librarians and trustees should accept this perspective simply because it is influential. The community movement perspective needs to be approached as a source of new ideas to be tested against real world problems. These ideas can be tested only when they are understood.

Looking through a New Lens

Whereas paradigms help people to focus and structure their view of the world, they do so by drawing attention away from certain aspects of the world that are deemed less important. This necessary mode of operation makes the choice of paradigms extremely important. Once a person has chosen to view the world through a certain lens, it may no longer be possible to see what the lens does not reveal. Extreme individualism, for example, makes it difficult to see the social dimension of life. In his book *A New World Waiting to Be Born: Civility Rediscovered*, M. Scott Peck describes the inability to perceive the social dimension of life as "a hole in the mind" that afflicts American culture. Peck notes that the American preoccupation with individual life has blinded people to the needs of the social structures that support individual life.[6]

The 1985 classic *Habits of the Heart: Individualism and Commitment in American Life* by Robert Bellah and his associates was immensely influential in developing the worldview of the community movement. Bellah provides historical perspective on America's intensely individualistic culture by analyzing contemporary cultural life in the light of remarks about American culture made 150 years earlier by French social philosopher Alexis de Tocqueville in his book *Democracy in America*.

> Tocqueville depicted the conflicts between the democratic citizen's concern for individual advancement and security on the one hand and religion and local political participation on the other. He traced privatizing tendencies to the new spirit of individualism attendant on nascent commercial capitalism and concern for community to the republican and biblical traditions.[7]

In describing the emptiness of radical individualism, Bellah and his colleagues remind people that Americans live within a social context despite a cultural inability to acknowledge this obvious truth.

We believe that much of the thinking about the self of educated Americans, thinking that has become almost hegemonic in our universities and much of the middle class, is based on inadequate social science, impoverished philosophy, and vacuous theology. There are truths we do not see when we adopt the language of radical individualism. We find ourselves not independently of other people and institutions but through them. We never get to the bottom of our selves on our own. We discover who we are face to face and side by side with others in work, love, and learning. All of our activity goes on in relationships, groups, associations, and communities ordered by institutional structures and interpreted by cultural patterns of meaning. Our individualism is itself one such pattern. And the positive side of our individualism, our sense of the dignity, worth, and moral autonomy of the individual, is dependent in a thousand ways on a social, cultural, and institutional context that keeps us afloat even when we cannot very well describe it.[8]

One of the many strengths of *Habits of the Heart: Individualism and Commitment in American Life* is that the authors utilize a number of case studies to illustrate their concerns. Examining the social commitments of a number of individuals helps to show the limitations of the paradigm of the autonomous individual.

It is possible to find a sense of perspective from a more recent historical past than Alexis de Tocqueville's visit to America in the 1830s. A great deal can be learned by simply recalling the cultural life of the 1950s, a period in which the ideas of Romanticism were much less powerful in the nation's culture. In his book *The Lost City: Discovering the Forgotten Virtues of Community in the Chicago of the 1950s*, Alan Ehrenhalt examines this lost world to place the current cultural paradigm in perspective.

> Most of us in America believe a few simple propositions that seem so clear and self-evident they scarcely need to be said.
> Choice is a good thing in life, and the more of it we have, the happier we are. Authority is inherently suspect; nobody should have the right to tell others what to think or how to behave. Sin isn't personal, it's social; individual human beings are creatures of the society they live in.
> Those ideas could stand as the manifesto of an entire generation in America, the generation born in the baby-boom years and now in its thirties and forties. They are powerful ideas. They all have the ring of truth. But in the past quarter-century, taken to excess, they have caused a great deal of trouble.
> The worship of choice has brought us a world of restless dissatisfaction, in which nothing we choose seems good enough to be permanent and we are unable to resist the endless pursuit of new selections—in

work, in marriage, in front of the television set. The suspicion of authority has meant the erosion of standards of conduct and civility, visible
most clearly in schools where teachers who dare to discipline pupils risk
a profane response. The repudiation of sin has given us a collection of
wrongdoers who insist that they are not responsible for their actions because they have been dealt bad cards in life. When we declare that there
are no sinners, we are a step away from deciding that there is no such
thing as right and wrong.

We have grown fond of saying that there is no free lunch, but we forget that it applies in moral as well as economic terms. Stable relationships, civil classrooms, safe streets—the ingredients of what we call
community—all come at a price. The price is limits on the choices we
can make as individuals, rules and authorities who can enforce them, and
a willingness to accept the fact that there are bad people in the world and
that sin exists in even the best of us. The price is not low, but the life it
makes possible is no small achievement.[9]

This section from *The Lost City* is one of the most concise statements of the community movement perspective. In this passage Alan
Ehrenhalt touches on a wide range of community movement concerns
including the relationship of social order to individual liberty, the need
for social authority in the areas of education and morality, and the importance of effective, responsible decision making for individuals and
the society as a whole. Americans need to remember what life was like
before the cultural civil war. This lost world should be remembered, but
not for the purpose of re-creating it. This is neither possible nor desirable. It should be remembered because it contained elements needed to
construct the future, elements that are almost invisible to the current
worldview.

The new cultural lens of the community movement is a lens that sees
the social context of individual life and seeks to protect this fragile social ecology. As social animals, human beings depend upon the intricate web of social connections just as they depend upon the natural
ecological systems of the planet. Americans cannot protect such endangered social systems as families, neighborhoods, schools, and communities, however, if people do not see these structures or do not understand the importance of these structures.

In his book *Childhood's Future*, Richard Louv describes the web of
social connections.

We have heard much in recent years of society's safety net. We have
been assured by some politicians that it was intact and all was well, that
anyone who fell through would be caught. But it is clear today that, given
current trends, the safety net cannot hold. I have therefore come to think

of the overall environmental pattern in this way: visualize, above the safety net, a great network, a supportive and intricate web. This web is far more important than the safety net, yet we pay much less attention to it, to patching it and simply respecting it. It is a wonderfully intricate and liberating web, and not easily described or quantified or fixed through fad legislation. One strand, the most important, is made of parents; another is the school system; another is the work place and how it treats parents; another is the neighborhood; another is how the city is shaped.[10]

He later notes that, "Once the web begins to unravel, the smallest bodies fall through first."[11]

When people allow themselves to clearly see the social world around them, they can begin to understand that world; they can begin to strengthen the social structures necessary for the health and welfare of individual citizens.

Social Authority: Balancing Rights and Responsibilities

Once people see the social environment and acknowledge the support received from this complex web of social relationships, it becomes clear that the pursuit of individual rights must be balanced with the individual's responsibility to support social structures. The extent to which rights and responsibilities are out of balance in the current culture and strategies to resolve this imbalance are major topics of two extremely important books by sociologist Amitai Etzioni, *The Spirit of Community: The Reinvention of American Society* and *The New Golden Rule: Community and Morality in a Democratic Society*. In these books Etzioni helps Americans to think through the intellectual, political, social, and public policy implications of the paradigm offered by the community movement. In this section on social authority, Etzioni's view of the current imbalance between rights and responsibilities will be described. The section will conclude by describing the implications of this perspective for education and social morality.

The Imbalance between Rights and Responsibilities

Amitai Etzioni describes the imbalance of rights and responsibilities by citing a study showing that although young Americans believe it is their right to receive a jury trial if they are accused of a crime, many do not feel that they have a civic duty to serve on a jury.[12] Etzioni describes the ethical dimension of the imbalance between rights and responsibilities in the following manner. "To take and not to give is an amoral, self-centered predisposition that ultimately no society can tolerate." In noting that "rights presume responsibilities," Etzioni reminds Americans of an important and self-evident reality that is apparently not seen through the paradigm of radical individualism.[13]

By showing the interdependency of rights and responsibilities, Etzioni demonstrates a critical flaw in today's culture war between the civil libertarians of the Left and social conservatives of the Right. Arguing for a society of unlimited rights leads toward anarchism. Arguing for a society of unlimited responsibilities leads toward authoritarianism. Both of these options are profoundly undemocratic. The communitarian approach requires a balancing of rights and responsibilities, of social order and individual liberty. This balancing assumes that basing a society entirely upon either social order or individual liberty will not result in a healthy society.[14]

Radical individualists believe that their views are exactly opposite to the views of authoritarians, who would support totalitarian government. In a strange way, however, the politics of anarchism and authoritarianism are closely related. Just as antisocial Romanticism based upon the ideas of Rousseau contributed to the rise of fascism in the twentieth century through the idea of the "general will," anarchy, as an extreme level of social disorder, may be the quickest route to authoritarianism. Etzioni reminds us that when basic physical safety is not assured it is common for people to "call for stronger and stronger police measures, and ultimately for 'strong leaders.'"[15] It is clear that a society without structure, which offers rights unbounded by responsibilities, is a Romantic fantasy that cannot be achieved. The pursuit of this dream can, however, succeed in undermining the brilliantly practical, though demanding, process of democracy that was set into motion by America's Founding Fathers.

Etzioni explains that "a good society does not favor the social good over individual choices or vice versa; it favors societal formations that serve the two dual social virtues in careful equilibrium."[16] By describing the need to find an equilibrium between rights and responsibilities, Amitai Etzioni has provided a conceptualization that clarifies both the genius of American democracy and the destructiveness of the challenges to democracy from the Right and Left that fuel cultural warfare.

The Communitarian Approach to Social Authority in Education and Morality

Communitarians support society's authority to educate and teach moral values by supporting both the validity and usefulness of knowledge and the moral right of educators to influence the lives of individuals. Both the validity of knowledge and society's right to influence the individual have been powerfully challenged by Romanticism via modernism and the counterculture. As Isaiah Berlin noted, the Romantics were implacably opposed to the idea of "reality as having some kind of form which could be studied, learnt, communicated to others, and in other respects treated in a scientific manner."[17] As E. D. Hirsch Jr. noted, "Romanticism believed that human nature was innately good, and should therefore be encouraged to take its natural course, unspoiled by the artificial impositions of social prejudice and convention."[18] This section will include a response to the challenge to the validity of knowledge, a discussion of society's right to educate individuals, and an analysis of the social importance of moral education.

Knowledge and the Necessity of Making Decisions

The extreme reluctance of Romanticism to accept any sense of certitude in the pursuit of truth is reflected in the type of relativism or "openness" that Allan Bloom criticizes in *The Closing of the American Mind*. Education does not make sense unless it is a search for better ways to think and live. The democratic process relies on education to help individuals and the society as a whole to make good decisions. When knowledge is challenged to the degree it is challenged by radical individualism, people have little confidence that truth, however qualified, can be either known or applied. As Isaiah Berlin noted, "to the extent to which not everything which science says is nonsense, not everything which common sense declares is untrue . . . romanticism . . . seems to me to be fallacious."[19] The tradition of undercutting confidence in knowledge and decision making has had a debilitating impact on American culture.

An odd thing about the openness of intellectual and moral relativism is that, as Allan Bloom explains, it actually closes the mind to accepting any particular position in the name of opening the mind to the tolerance of all possibilities. This position is equivalent to deciding not to decide. Under the pressure of everyday life, an intellectual and moral vacuum of this type can, of course, not be sustained. Bloom explains that "whatever is most powerful" in the culture will enter this vacuum.[20]

The Right and Necessity of Society to Educate Individuals

A society clearly deserves socially responsible behavior from individuals in exchange for the benefits that society offers. Society has the authority and the obligation to educate its young. The communitarian approach depends largely upon education to encourage citizens to accept their duties as members of democratic communities. The education of free individuals is viewed as a legitimate and absolutely necessary social function. Sharing knowledge that is structured by society, knowledge that includes the core moral values of society, should be done vigorously, but with the opportunity for individuals to reject these core values. The communitarian approach opposes both the positive view of indoctrination offered by the social conservatives of the Right and the opposition to the most modest efforts to socialize the young that is characteristic of the civil libertarian Left.

Although it ought to be obvious, many Americans no longer understand the importance of society's efforts to provide education. This is especially true in the case of moral education relating to character development and citizenship. It is clear that one aspect of the social deterioration that followed the counterculture has been a sharp decline in public support for public education. In his book *Is There a Public for Public Schools?*, David Mathews noted in 1994 that an alarming implication of ten years of Kettering Foundation research had been the "erosion of the historic commitment to the idea of schools for the benefit of the entire community." He finds that effective school reform will require reconnecting the public to its schools.[21] Although the Kettering Foundation and many other social scientists look for the reasons for this problem in a myriad of socioeconomic trends, it is clear that the pervasive belief that society does not have the authority to educate is at the heart of this disconnect.

Society's authority to educate the individual is, as noted earlier, central to both the Founding Fathers' conception of American democracy and to the conception of the public library as developed by the trustees of Boston Public Library in 1852. The necessity of society's educational function was affirmed by America's great philosopher of education John Dewey in his 1916 classic *Democracy and Education: An Introduction to the Philosophy of Education*.

Society exists through a process of transmission quite as much as biological life. This transmission occurs by means of communication of habits of doing, thinking, and feeling from the older to the younger. Without this communication of ideals, hopes, expectations, standards, opinions, from those members of society who are passing out of the group life to those who are coming into it, social life could not survive.[22]

To radical individualists influenced by Romanticism via modernism and the counterculture, the death of society may seem to be the liberation of the individual. In fact, as community movement writers have noted, the individual cannot thrive without a healthy social environment.

The rejection of society's right to educate the individual was a central tenet of the counterculture and the New Left. The popularity in the late 1960s and early 1970s of such works as *Deschooling Society* by Ivan Illich, the many books on education by John Holt, and A. S. Neill's classic *Summerhill: A Radical Approach to Child Rearing* make it clear that the counterculture and New Left supported Rousseau's opposition to education as a means of socializing the individual. Illich forthrightly advocated abolishing public schools. In his book *Escape from Childhood: The Needs and Rights of Children*, John Holt rails not only against compulsory education, but against any limitation on the rights of children based upon their age.

By now I have come to feel that the fact of being a "child," of being wholly subservient and dependent, of being seen by older people as a mixture of expensive nuisance, slave, and super-pet, does most young people more harm than good.

I propose instead that the rights, privileges, duties, responsibilities of adult citizens be made *available* to any young person, of whatever age, who wants to make use of them.[23]

Holt's extreme position is an echo of the ideas of A. S. Neill in *Summerhill*, which, in turn, echoed Rousseau. Neill argues, "To give freedom is to allow the child to live his own life. Thus expressed, it seems simple. Only our disastrous habit of teaching and molding and lecturing and coercing renders us incapable of realizing the simplicity of true freedom."[24]

Although these antieducational positions are extreme, they have been highly influential. The traditional idea of education as socialization is now a minority position among today's educators according to Kay S. Hymowitz.

A study from the research group Public Agenda found that only 7% of education professors think teachers should be "conveyors of knowledge who enlighten students with what they know." Ninety-two percent believe teachers should only "enable students to learn on their own." In the current argot, teachers are not even supposed to be teachers. They are "facilitators," "managers of instruction," or "coaches." Seymour Papert, author of *The Children's Machine*, views teachers as "co-learners"; in some schools, students even grade them in "reverse report cards."[25]

The idea that human nature and culture will thrive without the active social transmission of both complex types of knowledge and core values is, of course, untrue as John Dewey has explained.

The primary ineluctable facts of birth and death of each one of the constituent members in a social group determine the necessity of education. On one hand, there is the contrast between the immaturity of the newborn members of the group—its future sole representatives—and the maturity of the adult members who possess the knowledge and customs of the group. On the other hand, there is the necessity that these immature members be not merely physically preserved in adequate numbers, but that they be initiated into the interests, purposes, information, skill, and practices of the mature members: otherwise the group will cease its characteristic life. Even in a savage tribe, the achievements of adults are far beyond what the immature members would be capable of if left to themselves. With the growth of civilization, the gap between the original capacities of the immature and the standards and customs of the elders increases. Mere physical growing up, mere mastery of the bare necessities of subsistence will not suffice to reproduce the life of the group. Deliberate effort and the taking of thoughtful pains are required. Beings who are born not only unaware of, but quite indifferent to, the aims and habits of the social group have to be rendered cognizant of them and actively interested. Education, and education alone, spans the gap.[26]

Raising the "Moral Voice" of the Community

Community movement thinkers such as Etzioni make a powerful contribution to the topic of moral education in their strong reaffirmation of character development and civic education. The communitarian position on moral education seems, on the surface, to support the position of the social conservatives of the Right. This position is, however, very different from the position of the social conservatives and much more appealing to the rest of the culture. Etzioni notes that for social life to be sustained and transmitted to the next generation a community must raise its "moral voice."[27] Although any sort of moral pronounce-

ment from society is viewed as authoritarian by expressive individualists, it is entirely appropriate to reinforce society's moral values in a
democratic context. Etzioni notes that the alternatives to a community
that exercises its moral voice are unacceptably undemocratic.

> The fact that those voices are to be raised in moderation, and only in
> ways that do not violate overarching values, should not hide the fact that
> we cannot be a civil or decent society without a moral voice. Ask your-
> self what the alternatives are to the exercise of moral voices. There are
> only two: a police state, which tries to maintain civic order by brute
> force, or a moral vacuum in which anything goes.[28]

America is beginning to strengthen its moral voice. This is greatly to be
preferred over building more prisons at the request of the political
Right while the political Left further weakens the nation's moral voice
and, in doing so, exacerbates social disorder.

The primary concern in raising the community's "moral voice" in an
educational setting is, of course, how to determine which values to
teach in a pluralistic society. Individualists who concentrate on the differences between people believe this to be an impossible task. Community movement thinkers, however, observe that there is more unanimity
concerning values than people generally recognize. Etzioni reminds
people that many values are shared by a wide range of ethnic and socioeconomic groups. "Nobody considers it moral to abuse children,
rape, steal (not to mention commit murder), be disrespectful of others,
discriminate, and so on." These shared values form a basis for social
order and must be communicated to the rising generation. Disputed
values, which are less common, can be taught from a variety of viewpoints.[29]

Society should actively reinforce shared values. It is not reasonable
to force everyone to accept the typical values of a Southern Baptist
living in the 1950s as many social conservatives propose. It is also not
reasonable to attempt to drive society's moral voice out of its remaining
influence as many expressive individualists propose. Society should
use education based upon shared moral values to maintain its strength.

Conclusion

Democratic education and social morality does not force people to
choose between individual freedom and social order, between relativism and absolutism, or between the laissez-faire nurturing of natural
impulses or military-style indoctrination. In each case these polarities

represent inappropriate extremes that will not in themselves provide a practical means for building a democratic society.

Individuals require social support. Real life is characterized neither by the complete uncertainty of relativism nor by the complete certainty of absolutism. It is about knowing some things and doing one's best to apply this limited knowledge to personal and social decisions. Education and social morality in a democratic society cannot succeed without society's vigorous work to provide a positive influence just as it cannot succeed through authoritarian coercion.

Community movement thinkers suggest a return to and fulfillment of the great tradition of democratic education by affirming the human capacity to know the world as well as society's authority and duty to transmit this knowledge to the individual. Although this has been the dominant view of education through much of our nation's history, this view is now seriously challenged. The future of our society depends upon a concerted effort to support good decision making through the social transmission of knowledge. This must be achieved in an environment that is respectful of the autonomy of the individual. The communitarian position is finding an educational balance that honors both individual liberty and the need for social order. To quote philosopher John Dewey in describing education in a democratic society, "Such a society must have a type of education which gives individuals a personal interest in social relationships and control, and the habits of mind which secure social changes without introducing disorder."[30]

Building Communities: Social Morality and Civility, Civic Infrastructure, Dialogue and Common Ground, and Collaboration

In this section, an outline of the recurring themes in community movement literature related to building communities will be presented. As noted in earlier sections, the community movement believes that there needs to be a balance between individual rights and responsibilities and that contemporary America places too much stress on rights and too little stress on responsibilities. Unlike radical individualists, community movement thinkers believe that society has the authority and the duty to educate individuals concerning their social obligations as well as their rights. Although community movement literature addresses these basic issues of social philosophy, much of the literature of the movement is directed toward the specific strategies for building communities.

As community movement literature is extensive and varied in approach, this introduction can offer only a small sample of these ideas. The intent here is to list some of the prominent themes of this literature and to provide sample quotations that demonstrate these themes. The true power and usefulness of this literature can be understood only through a first hand exploration of the books quoted here and the many other books and articles on related topics.

Social Morality and Civility

A basic project of the community movement has been to rebuild the culture's interest in and respect for social morality. Among other related issues, the community movement has discussed social morality as a philosophical issue, as an educational topic, as a matter of personal manners, and as a means of improving race relations.

James Q. Wilson's 1993 book *The Moral Sense* made a powerful contribution to the philosophical discussion of social morality. He explains that Aristotle, Thomas Aquinas, and even Adam Smith understood that mankind is naturally motivated by moral concerns related to membership in a society as well as by strictly personal concerns.[31] He notes that modern philosophy, however, has withdrawn support for that view.

> Modern philosophy, with some exceptions, represents a fundamental break with that tradition. For the last century or so, few of the great philosophical theories of human behavior have accorded much weight to the possibility that men and women are naturally endowed with anything remotely resembling a moral sense.[32]

Wilson explains that, in addition to pre-modern Western traditions that still exert influence, human nature itself works powerfully against the amoral perspective of radical individualism.

> There can scarcely be anything worth calling a moral sense if people can be talked out of it by modern philosophy, secular humanism, Marxist dialectics, or pseudo-Freudian psychoanalysis. But I doubt that most people most of the time are affected by these intellectual fashions. The intellectuals who consume them may be affected. If they think that life is without moral meaning, they may live accordingly, creating an avant-garde in which "meaning" is to be found in self-expressive art, a bohemian counterculture, or anarchistic politics. But the lives of most people

are centered around the enduring facts of human existence—coping with a family, establishing relationships, and raising children. Everywhere we look, we see ordinary men and women going about their affairs, happily or unhappily as their circumstances allow, making and acting on moral judgments without pausing to wonder what Marx or Freud or Rorty would say about those judgments. In the intimate realms of life, there will be stress, deprivation, and frustration, but ordinarily these will not be experienced as a pervasive spiritual crisis.[33]

Wilson's efforts to describe humanity's "moral sense" are highly practical as well as theoretical. He finds the modern inability to speak confidently of moral choices unnecessary and damaging to both individual and societal decision making.

It *is* a task of this book, however, to make us ask whether the mirror that modern skepticism has held up to mankind's face reflects what we wish to see. Do we really *want* to have the utterly malleable, slightly cynical, superficially tolerant, wholly transparent human nature that we claim to have? Are we prepared for the possibility that by behaving as if no moral judgments were possible we may create a world that more and more resembles our diminished moral expectations? We must be careful of what we think we are, because we may become that.[34]

James Q. Wilson presents his description of humanity's moral sense "to help people recover the confidence with which they once spoke of virtue and morality." He seeks "to reestablish the possibility and the reasonableness of speaking frankly and convincingly about moral choices."[35]

In addition to reconstructing the concept of a meaningful social morality, community movement writers as well as educators throughout the nation have become deeply interested in communicating social morality through character development and civic education in the schools. The renewal of character development and civic education was been a major thrust of the U.S. Department of Education as well as the Communitarian Network during in the 1990s. In recent years the state of Maryland and a number of other states have established aggressive programs to encourage public school students to develop social responsibility. Such programs often include requirements for service to the community through a variety of work opportunities. An extensive literature on character development and civic education is now available.

A renewed interest in civility has also accompanied this general interest in strengthening social morality. Stephen L. Carter's book *Civil-*

ity: Manners, Morals, and the Etiquette of Democracy offers a readable and profound treatment of this old topic that is once again fashionable.

> Civility, I shall argue, is the sum of the many sacrifices we are called to make for the sake of living together. When we pretend that we travel alone, we can also pretend that these sacrifices are unnecessary. Yielding to this very human instinct for self-seeking, I shall argue; is often immoral, and certainly should not be done without forethought. We should make sacrifices for others not simply because doing so makes social life easier (although it does), but as a signal of respect for our fellow citizens, marking them as full equals, both before the law and before God. Rules of civility are thus also rules of morality: it is morally proper to treat our fellow citizens with respect, and morally improper not to. Our crisis of civility, then, is part of a larger crisis of morality.[36]

Stephen Carter, himself an African American, stresses the importance of a shared sense of social morality and civility in improving race relations.[37] This is a major concern among communitarian thinkers who find the fragmentation of groups in America to be as troubling as the rise of extreme individualism. If no basic framework of social morality can be agreed upon, groups have no basis for communication and society has no hope of order and coherence. Divisive forms of multiculturalism that propose a variety of entirely separate ethnic Americas are opposed. Communitarians echo the concerns of Arthur Schlesinger Jr. in this book *The Disuniting of America: Reflections on a Multicultural Society.*

> If we now repudiate the quite marvelous inheritance that history bestows on us, we invite the fragmentation of the national community into a quarrelsome spatter of enclaves, ghettos, tribes. The bonds of cohesion in our society are sufficiently fragile, or so it seems to me, that it makes no sense to strain them by encouraging and exalting cultural and linguistic apartheid.
>
> The American identity will never be fixed and final; it will always be in the making. Changes in the population have always brought changes in the national ethos and will continue to do so; but not, one must hope, at the expense of national integration. The question America confronts as a pluralistic society is how to vindicate cherished cultures and traditions without breaking the bonds of cohesion—common ideals, common political institutions, common language, common culture, common fate—that hold the republic together.[38]

Communitarians propose that group autonomy be balanced with the requirements of the overarching "community of communities." They agree that the "melting pot" concept is inappropriate because it tends to obliterate important and enriching cultural differences. They prefer to use the image of a "mosaic." Amitai Etzioni explains that a mosaic requires not only diverse elements, but "a frame and glue" to hold it together. He describes this approach as "pluralism within unity."[39]

Civic Infrastructure

In addition to providing an intellectual infrastructure that supports social morality, the community movement is deeply concerned with the problems of strengthening the social infrastructure that is needed to support the social and civic life of the community. The increased isolation of individuals, the alienation from civic life, and the fragmentation of society into hostile factions are pervasive problems that require a variety of interrelated solutions. Important themes in this area of communitarian literature include the need to strengthen the institutions of civil society, the need for civic space to enhance community identity and dialogue, and the need for new approaches to community planning and zoning.

Benjamin Barber defines civil society in the following manner in his book *A Place for Us: How to Make Society Civil and Democracy Strong.*

> In an ideal civic architecture of free nations, the space that accommodates the mutuality of "you and me" is civil society. The very phrase suggests an independent domain of free social life where neither governments nor private markets are sovereign; a realm we create for ourselves through associated common action in families, clans, churches, and communities; a "third sector" (the other two are the state and the market that mediates between our specific individuality as economic producers and consumers and our abstract collectivity as members of a sovereign people. The philosopher Michael Walzer's spare language calls civil society "the space of uncoerced human association and also the set of relational networks— formed for the sake of family, faith, interest and ideology—that fill this space."[40]

Community movement writers are concerned that the role of civil society has been downplayed in contemporary society as both government and the private sector have increased their domination of various aspects of American life. These writers find this disturbing because they understand that the civil sector is the generator of social morality. If the civil sector is weakened, they reason, a society's social morality will also be weakened. This is why the community movement is so interested in collaboration with churches and other institutions of civil society in solving social problems.

Benjamin Barber expresses the community movement's concern that our current society does not provide adequate civic space to foster community identity and dialogue.

> Without civil society, citizens are homeless: suspended between big bureaucratic governments which they no longer trust . . . and private markets they cannot depend on for moral and civic values. . . . The "commons" vanishes, and where the public square once stood, there are only shopping malls and theme parks and not a single place that welcomes the "us" that we might hope to gather from all the private you's and me's.[41]

Although this statement may exaggerate the problem, it is clear that American society no longer recognizes the need for or provides for adequate civic space. Providing civic space is vital to the support of civil society. A recent trend is the development of virtual civic space on the Internet in the form of electronic discussion groups devoted to community life and public issues.

The need for a new approach to community planning and zoning is also an important topic in community movement literature. James Howard Kunstler has written two influential books on combating the anticommunitarian impact of urban sprawl, *The Geography of Nowhere* and *Home from Nowhere: Remaking Our Everyday World for the 21st Century*. His ideas have contributed to an architectural reform movement known as the Congress for the New Urbanism.

> The New Urbanism aims to reinstate the primacy of the public realm in American life. . . . The physical form that the New Urbanists envision is at once deeply familiar and revolutionary: the mixed-use neighborhood in increments of villages, towns, and cities. It is familiar because it is the way America built itself through most of our history, really until the end of World War Two. It is a physical form that complies exactly with many Americans' most cherished notions about our nation at its best. And yet the New Urbanism is revolutionary because it starkly contradicts the world of suburban sprawl that has become the real setting for our national life, and the source of so many of our woes. In doing so, the New Urbanism contradicts most established rules and methods for building things, particularly our zoning laws.
>
> This movement, in my view, is one of the most hopeful developments on the national scene. I share the belief of its members that if we can repair the physical fabric of our everyday world, many of the damaged and abandoned institutions of our civic life may follow into restoration. If

nothing else, I think we stand to regain places to live and work that are worthy of affection. And since a great many good things proceed from affection, I believe some of our desired social aims might naturally follow.[42]

Dialogue and Common Ground

The communitarian approach to developing social order depends heavily upon noncoercive means to develop a shared sense of morality and purpose. In addition to education, a great stress is placed upon public dialogue. Dialogue requires civility, attentive listening, and a real effort to find practical solutions that can be generally supported. Strategies for effective public dialogue abound in the literature of the community movement. One influential book that has helped to improve public dialogue is Deborah Tannen's *The Argument Culture: Stopping America's War of Words.*

> This book is about a pervasive warlike atmosphere that makes us approach public dialogue, and just about anything we need to accomplish, as if it were a fight. It is a tendency in Western culture in general, and in the United States in particular, that has a long history and a deep, thick, and far-ranging root system. It has served us well in many ways but in recent years has become so exaggerated that it is getting in the way of solving our problems. Our spirits are corroded by living in an atmosphere of unrelenting contention—an argument culture.
>
> The argument culture urges us to approach the world—and the people in it—in an adversarial frame of mind. It rests on the assumption that opposition is the best way to get anything done: The best way to discuss an idea is to set up a debate; the best way to cover the news is to find spokespeople who express the most extreme, polarized views and present them as "both sides;" the best way to settle disputes is litigation that pits one party against the other; the best way to show you're really thinking is to criticize.[43]

Tannen notes that, "Public discourse requires *making* an argument for a point of view, not *having* an argument—as in having a fight."[44] Her insightful book demonstrates strategies for developing a healthy dialogue that leads to common understandings and practical solutions.

As effective dialogue is based on sound knowledge, journalists interested in promoting dialogue as a means of building community have developed an influential new approach to their profession known as "civic" or "public" journalism. Public journalism seeks to focus the efforts of journalists on assisting the public in solving its problems through effective dialogue and decision making. Jay Rosen, a leading advocate of public journalism, describes this new approach in the following manner.

> Public journalism is an approach to the daily business of the craft that calls on journalists to (1) address people as citizens, potential participants in public affairs, rather than victims or spectators; (2) help the political community act upon, rather than just learn about, its problems; (3) improve the climate of public discussion, rather than simply watch it deteriorate; and (4) help make public life go well, so that it earns its claim on our attention. If journalists can find a way to do these things, they may in time restore public confidence in the press, reconnect with an audience that has been drifting away, rekindle the idealism that brought many of them into the craft and contribute, in a more substantial fashion, to the health of American democracy, which is the reason we afford journalists their many privileges and protections.[45]

Collaboration

A natural outgrowth of finding common ground through effective public dialogue is collaboration to solve community problems. The process of collaboration can be viewed as strengthening the web of community that supports both individuals and groups. The underlying logic here is that broad social problems cannot be solved by the fragmented efforts of specialized groups. The need for a comprehensive, integrated approach has been described by the adage "It takes a village to raise a child," a concept Hillary Clinton used in a popular book about supporting children. This concept of collaboration has been effectively used in a number of areas of social service, most notably law enforcement. "Community policing," a strategy for integrating police officers into the life of the neighborhoods they serve, has had a powerful influence upon communities throughout the nation during the 1990s.

Community movement thinkers have a special interest in involving the institutions of civil society, such as the churches, in these new collaborative efforts. This is due to the special place these institutions hold in the development and maintenance of social morality as well as the fact that these institutions have been wastefully underutilized in recent years.

Lisbeth B. Schorr documents a large number of effective partnerships in her book *Common Purpose: Strengthening Families and Neighborhoods to Rebuild America*. In dealing with poverty in America, Schorr gives the following advice.

Forget about choosing between bottom-up and top-down approaches. Depleted inner-city neighborhoods cannot turn themselves around without very substantial help from outside the neighborhood. But neither can outsiders impose solutions. Effective neighborhood transformation requires that community-based organizations be able to draw on funding, expertise, and influence from outside, and that outsiders be able to draw on information, expertise, and wisdom that can come only from the neighborhood itself.[46]

Schorr notes an important trend toward determining the accountability of social programs by measuring results or "outcomes."

Information about outcomes enables communities to be more deliberate in support of shared purposes. "In the long run, men hit only what they aim at," said Henry David Thoreau. Agreement on a common set of goals and outcomes helps to promote a community-wide "culture of responsibility" for children and families and spurs momentum for change. The rallying cry for investment in early intervention and prevention—such as when police chiefs advocate early education and expanded recreation opportunities to prevent youth crime—becomes more credible when investments can be reliably linked to outcomes.[47]

The strategy of collaboration to solve social problems recognizes the need to involve the whole community in the solution of major social problems. This strategy has resulted in countless successful experiments in alliances among government, private sector, and civil sector organizations during the 1990s. Broad collaboration to solve social problems may be the most immediate contribution of the community movement to American society. Collaborative efforts are most effective when informed by an understanding of the larger context of community movement ideas.

General Contributions of the Community Movement Perspective to American Society

Since roughly 1965, American society has undergone a period of great cultural disorientation and disintegration. This period appears to have ended sometime during the mid-1990s. The extreme individualism of the 1980s began to wane and a new concern for social responsibility emerged. The community movement can be viewed as both a cause and a reflection of this deep social transformation. American society is finding its balance again after years of confusion and cultural conflict.

A new unity of purpose is beginning to transcend political gridlock and cultural warfare. American society is becoming stronger and more coherent as it finds a new balance between individual autonomy and social order. Evidence is mounting that this cultural shift is underway and that a new spirit of optimism is transforming American society.

Sociological and Political Evidence that the Perspective of the Community Movement Is Transforming American Society

Francis Fukuyama and E. J. Dionne Jr. provide sociological and political evidence that this important and beneficial cultural shift has begun. In his book *The Great Disruption: Human Nature and the Reconstitution of Social Order*, Francis Fukuyama provides important sociological evidence that the renewal of social norms of behavior is underway.

> Evidence is growing that the Great Disruption has run its course and that the process of renorming has already begun. Rates of increase in crime, divorce, illegitimacy, and distrust have slowed substantially and even reversed in the 1990s. . . . This is particularly the case in the United States, where levels of crime have fallen more than 15 percent from the peak levels of the early 1990s. Divorce rates peaked in the early 1980s, and the proportion of births to single mothers has stopped increasing. . . . Levels of trust in both institutions and individuals have also recovered significantly form the early to the late 1990s.[48]

E. J. Dionne Jr. describes the renewed interest in balancing individual autonomy and social order in his book *They Only Look Dead: Why Progressives Will Dominate the Next Political Era*. Dionne notes that the libertarian political direction of the country peaked with the Republican Party's 1994 "Contract with America" and went into decline in 1995 when Clinton won the standoff over the approval of the federal budget.

> The revolt against Progressivism is becoming the dominant political project of the Republican Party.
> It is the central argument of this book that this attack, far from routing Progressivism, is a precursor of its renewal. For two decades, Progressives have been timid in defending their project, and distracted by cultural politics. The Gingrich Revolution gives them no choice but to battle to preserve Progressivism's achievements and renew its program. And as support for the Republican Congress dropped in the autumn of 1995, it

became clear many voters were, indeed, looking for more from government than Gingrich wanted to offer. *Especially* if Gingrich is right about
the vast technological changes that are coming, it is highly unlikely that
the central thrust of American politics will be toward dismantling the
buffers that ease change and the social protections that ease suffering. By
moving American conservatism toward a rendezvous with nineteenth
century laissez-faire doctrines, Gingrich and his allies will force their op-
ponents to grapple with the task of constructing the twenty-first-century
alternatives to laissez-faire.[49]

The extreme individualism of libertarian politics has been less strident since the Republican budget defeat of 1995. Although libertarian
politics continues to hold power in the Republican Party, Republican
presidential candidates George W. Bush and John McCain waged campaigns for the 2000 election that were friendlier to government than the
militant antigovernment rhetoric of Newt Gingrich in 1995. George W.
Bush stressed that he has the ability to unify diverse groups of people
while John McCain reached out to independent voters with moderate
positions on issues such as campaign finance reform. Antigovernment
rhetoric has been tempered to match the public's increased confidence
in government during recent years. People now believe that social progress can be made because they have seen positive results from governmental policies relating to economic growth and a wide range of other
issues.

Since 1992 the Clinton administration has initiated and developed a
powerful redefinition of the progressive tradition by promoting the
communitarian philosophy and legislative agenda of the Democratic
Leadership Council. E. J. Dionne Jr. confirms the progressive nature of
the Clinton agenda. He states that

> the intellectual spirit behind the New Democrat project as conceived by
> its authors in the Democratic Leadership council had been not conserva-
> tive but *progressive* in spirit. The DLC named its think tank the Progres-
> sive Policy Institute precisely to make clear its allegiance to the tradition
> of the Roosevelts and Woodrow Wilson.[50]

The reorientation of the Democratic Party along the communitarian,
progressive lines of the Democratic Leadership Council has been so
successful that the approach was adopted by Tony Blair in Great Britain to revitalize the Labour Party.

Both in terms of sociological and political change, there is evidence
that America is entering a new era of social order and coherence, a new
progressive era. This cultural shift is moving the nation away from lib-

ertarian individualism toward a communitarian understanding of the need to balance individual liberty and social order.

Optimism Based on Realism and Positive Results

The perspective of the community movement offers the optimism and excitement of finding a new path toward fulfillment. This is not, however, the optimism and excitement of knowing exactly what to do or the optimism and excitement of freedom without social constraints. The optimism of the community movement perspective is more tempered because it is truer to the mixture of limitation and potentiality inherent in the human condition.

Jedediah Purdy describes this type of optimism in his book *For Common Things: Irony, Trust, and Commitment in America Today.*

> In dedicating ourselves, in accepting responsibility, we cultivate a special quality of perception. This is the habit of seeing things in their complex mutual dependence, and understanding how what we most value is implicated in that web. The corollary of recognizing dependence in this way is a sense of gratitude and wonder that so much has gone into the upkeep of what sustains and delights us. In this condition, sometimes, understanding and wonder can grow together. This is at the same time a way to sobering recognition of our capacity for destruction, and of the potency of neglect.[51]

The perspective Purdy describes does not promise simple solutions. It offers the opportunity to make a contribution to solving the complex problems of the real world.

> We need today a kind of thought and action that is too little contemplated yet remains possible. It is the kind aimed at the preservation of what we love most in the world, and a stay against forgetting what that love requires. It is an exercise of margins against boundlessness, of earned hope against casual despair, and of responsibility against heedlessness.[52]

The community movement calls for a return to the hard, but real work of democracy. The community movement encourages people to embrace both the limits and the possibilities of what can be done to improve the lives of the American people.

The realistic optimism of the community movement perspective stands in striking contrast to the unrealistic promises of expressive individualism. The euphoria elicited by Romanticism's promise of unlimited freedom is followed by Romantic despair when this promise is not realized. As Isaiah Berlin describes this process, "the romantics tend to oscillate between extremes of mystical optimism and appalling pessimism. . . ."[53] In our era, the New Left promised that withdrawing support from "the system" would result in a perfect community of individual freedom. When this hope of Romantic anarchism was not realized, a darker, much more pessimistic view prevailed. This pessimism blends well with the harsh ethos of Right-wing libertarianism. It lives on in numerous cultural forms. A notable form of this pessimism is found in the more depressing forms of alternative music, which are dedicated to youthful angst and despair. Another form of this pessimism is the cynicism and ironic perspective criticized by Jedediah Purdy. He describes the relationship between unrealistic hopes and disillusionment.

> We live in a disappointed aftermath of a politics that aspired to change the human predicament in elemental ways, but whose hopes have resolved into heavy disillusionment. We have difficulty trusting the speech and thought that we might use to try to make sense of our situation. We have left behind an unreal hope to fall into a hopelessness that is inattentive to and mistrustful of reality. What we might hope for now is a culture able to approach its circumstances with attention and care, and a politics that, as part of a broader responsibility for common things, turns careful attention into caring practice.[54]

Purdy describes his hopeful philosophy as paying attention to reality and doing what can be done. The optimism of the community movement perspective is that reality offers possibilities for success and that people can work together to achieve success. Neither the expectation of perfection nor the despair that results when perfection is not achieved characterizes real life. To assume, as many have in recent decades, that society is utterly incapable of solving problems of any type is simply not true. Perfection is beyond human capabilities, but improvement is possible. This perspective encourages people to see life in its complexity, to balance the need for multiple social goods. It asks that the hard work of uniting people around shared goals be engaged and that the temptation to approach politics as simply a vehicle for individual or group expression be resisted. The community movement, like American democracy itself, is oriented toward making decisions and solving problems.

The optimism of the community movement is based on the idea that people can work together to improve society. This optimism has been reinforced by successful collaborative efforts to solve social problems.

The sharp drop in crime rates in cities such as Boston and New York during the 1990s has been widely acknowledged to be the result of using community policing strategies such as developing community-wide coalitions. During the period from June 1995 to June 1996, for example, the Dorchester section of Boston experienced a 29 percent drop in violent crime and a 21 percent drop in property crime that has been attributed to community policing.[55] Although successes have been achieved in solving a variety of social problems due to new community collaborations, community policing has been most impressive due to the seemingly intractable nature of urban crime and the sharp reductions in crime rates.

A New Cultural Maturity

C. G. Jung's commentary on *The Secret of the Golden Flower: A Chinese Book of Life* included the observation that, "the Chinese have never failed to recognize the paradoxes and the polarity inherent in what is alive. The opposites always balanced one another—a sign of high culture. One-sidedness, though it lends momentum, is a mark of barbarism."[56] The community movement perspective seeks to balance the individual and society, to balance rights and responsibilities. In doing so, it provides a more sophisticated model for human life than competing perspectives that promote a one-sided dedication to either individual autonomy or social order. Such a perspective is the type of cultural maturity that American culture needs to achieve.

Wendell Berry describes America's excessive individualism as a problem of cultural immaturity in his 1990 essay "Writer and Region."

> It is arguable, I think, that our country's culture is still suspended as if at the end of *Huckleberry Finn*, assuming that its only choices are either a deadly "civilization" of piety and violence or an escape into some "Territory" where we may remain free of adulthood and community obligation. We want to be free; we want to have rights; we want to have power; we do not yet want much to do with responsibility. We have imagined the great and estimable freedom of boyhood, of which Huck Finn remains the finest spokesman. We have imagined the bachelorhoods of nature and genius and power: the contemplative, the artist, the hunter, the cowboy, the general, the president—lives dedicated and solitary in the Territory of individuality. But boyhood and bachelorhood have remained our norms of "liberation," for women as well as men. We have hardly begun to imagine the coming to responsibility that is the meaning, and the liberation, of growing up. We have hardly begun to imagine community life, and the tragedy that is at the heart of community life.[57]

Berry defines the "beloved community" and the rarity of the depiction of such a community in American literature.

> This leads us, probably, to as good a definition of the beloved community as we can hope for: common experience and common effort on a common ground to which one willingly belongs. The life of such a community has been very little regarded in American literature. Our writers have been much more concerned with the individual who is misunderstood or mistreated by a community that is no sense beloved, as in *The Scarlet Letter*. From Thoreau to Hemingway and his successors, a great deal of sympathy and interest has been given to the individual as pariah or gadfly exile. In Faulkner, a community is the subject, but it is a community disintegrating, as it was doomed to do by the original sins of land greed, violent honor, and slavery. . . .
> The one American book I know that is about a beloved community—a settled, established white American community with a sustaining common culture, and mostly beneficent toward both its members and its place—is Sarah Orne Jewett's *The Country of the Pointed Firs*.[58]

The community movement perspective provides both inspiration to build the beloved community and strategies that allow this important work to succeed. The community movement reorients our culture to the work of democracy that has always been hard, but never impossible.

Conclusion

Community movement ideas have made a major contribution to ending cultural warfare and political gridlock. This new perspective has helped to begin the long process of renewing both the moral infrastructure and the social infrastructure of the nation. The community movement perspective renews the neglected tradition of building a unified, integrated nation from America's pluralistic moral and social fragments. The goal is to protect the autonomy of individuals and groups while developing a basic moral and social framework that everyone can support. This is not an easy process, but it is the process upon which the nation is founded and one that has so far proven itself superior to all challengers.

The community movement's ideas concerning the moral infrastructure, described here as relating to the concept of social authority, might be summarized by the following list.

- Human nature is a mixture of good and evil.
- Society needs to support good and suppress evil by educating individuals to make appropriate personal and social decisions.
- General agreement on issues of social morality can be achieved in many areas.
- Individual and group autonomy needs to be balanced with social order. Rights must balance responsibilities.
- Democracy requires the active involvement of all citizens in civic life, including participation in civic dialogue and voting as well as cooperation in solving social problems.

Although the details of this description of an appropriate moral infrastructure for democracy are often new and interesting, the basic framework corresponds with the ideas of the Founding Fathers. The importance of the community movement in the area of moral infrastructure has been to illustrate the strengths of the traditional moral framework of the democracy, to show how the nation has deviated from this framework, and to demonstrate how this framework can be used effectively in contemporary society.

Community movement ideas for rebuilding the social infrastructure provide practical strategies for using the moral infrastructure to strengthen society. These strategies have proven themselves to be powerful and effective, but, like democracy itself, they involve the hard work that is always required to solve complex problems. Community movement ideas for rebuilding the social infrastructure might be summarized by the following list.

- Strengthen the family and the other institutions of civil society, which together provide the foundation for social morality.
- Strengthen character development and civic education through a general effort to raise the "moral voice" of the community and through specific efforts in the schools.
- Promote a better understanding of community identity and issues through various forms of education and through civic journalism.
- Encourage civic dialogue by providing more opportunities for people to discuss community issues in face-to-face group meetings and online.
- Physically structure communities through planning and architecture in ways that promote civic interaction and social health.

- Establish constructive ground rules for civic dialogue, such as the requirement of civility, to promote an atmosphere conducive to finding common ground.
- Encourage collaborative efforts that include government, private sector, and civil sector groups in the solution of broad social problems. One example of this strategy has been the integration of law enforcement into community life through community policing.

A new spirit of optimism about social projects has developed thanks to the reduction of crime rates through community policing and other successful uses of community movement ideas. The cultural tide is turning away from extreme individualism and toward a renewed national commitment to strengthening our endangered social structures.

Notes

1. Amitai Etzioni, *The Spirit of Community: The Reinvention of American Society* (New York: Simon & Schuster, 1993), 12.

2. Isaiah Berlin, *The Roots of Romanticism* (Princeton: Princeton University Press, 1999), 117.

3. Etzioni, *Spirit of Community*, 2.

4. Joel Arthur Barker, *Paradigms: The Business of Discovering the Future* (New York: HarperCollins, 1992), 32.

5. E. D. Hirsch Jr., *The Schools We Need: And Why We Don't Have Them* (New York: Doubleday, 1996), 71.

6. M. Scott Peck, *A World Waiting to Be Born: Civility Rediscovered* (New York: Bantam Books, 1993), 32.

7. Robert N. Bellah et al., *Habits of the Heart: Individualism and Commitment in American Life* (Berkeley: University of California Press, 1996), 40.

8. Bellah, *Habits of the Heart*, 84.

9. Alan Ehrenhalt, *The Lost City: Discovering the Forgotten Virtues of Community in the Chicago of the 1950s* (New York: Basic Books, 1995), [2-3]

10. Richard Louv, *Childhood's Future* (Boston: Houghton Mifflin, 1990), 5-6.

11. Louv, *Childhood's Future*, 6.

12. Etzioni, *Spirit of Community*, 3.

13. Etzioni, *Spirit of Community*, 10, 9.

14. Amitai Etzioni, *The New Golden Rule: Community and Morality in a Democratic Society* (New York: Basic Books, 1996), 5.

15. Etzioni, *New Golden Rule*, 43.

16. Etzioni, *New Golden Rule*, 27.

17. Berlin, *Roots of Romanticism,* 127.

18. Hirsch, *Schools We Need,* 74.

19. Berlin, *Roots of Romanticism,* 146.

20. Allan Bloom, *The Closing of the American Mind* (New York: Simon & Schuster, 1987), 41.

21. David Mathews, *Is There a Public for Public Schools?* (Dayton, Ohio: Kettering Foundation Press, 1996), 2, 10.

22. John Dewey, *Democracy and Education: An Introduction to the Philosophy of Education* (New York: Free Press, 1944), 3.

23. John Holt, *Escape from Childhood* (New York: E. P. Dutton, 1974), 18.

24. A. S. Neill, *Summerhill: A Radical Approach to Child Rearing* (New York: Hart Publishing, 1960), 113.

25. Kay S. Hymowitz, *Ready or Not: Why Treating Children As Small Adults Endangers Their Future—and Ours* (New York: Free Press, 1999), 4.

26. Dewey, *Democracy and Education*, 3.

27. Etzioni, *Spirit of Community*, 23.

28. Etzioni, *Spirit of Community*, 37.

29. Etzioni, *Spirit of Community*, 99-100, 100.

30. Dewey, *Democracy and Education*, 99.

31. James Q. Wilson, *The Moral Sense* (New York: Free Press, 1993), 2.

32. Wilson, *Moral Sense,* 3.

33. Wilson, *Moral Sense,* 5.

34. Wilson, *Moral Sense,* x.

35. Wilson, *Moral Sense,* vii, vii.

36. Stephen L. Carter, *Civility: Manners, Morals, and the Etiquette of Democracy* (New York: Basic Books, 1998), 11.

37. Carter, *Civility*, 60-63.

38. Arthur M. Schlesinger Jr., *The Disuniting of America* (New York: Norton, 1992), 137-38.

39. Etzioni, *New Golden Rule*, 189, 192.

40. Benjamin Barber, *A Place for Us: How to Make Society Civil and Democracy Strong* (New York: Hill and Wang, 1998), 4.

41. Barber, *Place for Us,* 45.

42. James Howard Kunstler, *Home from Nowhere: Remaking Our Everyday World for the Twenty-First Century* (New York: Simon & Schuster, 1996), 19.

43. Deborah Tannen, *The Argument Culture: Stopping America's War of Words* (New York: Ballantine Books, 1998), 3.

44. Tannen, *Argument Culture*, 4.

45. Jay Rosen, "The Action of the Idea," in *The Idea of Public Journalism*, ed. Theodore L. Glasser (New York: Guilford Press, 1999), 22.

46. Lisbeth B. Schorr, *Common Purpose: Strengthening Families and Neighborhoods to Rebuild America* (New York: Anchor Books, 1997), 383.

47. Schorr, *Common Purpose*, 119.

48. Francis Fukuyama, *The Great Disruption: Human Nature and the Reconstitution of Social Order* (New York: Free Press, 1999), 119.

49. E. J. Dionne Jr., *They Only Look Dead: Why Progressives Will Dominate the Next Political Era* (New York: Simon & Schuster, 1996), 228-29.

50. Dionne, *They Only Look Dead,* 279.

51. Jedediah Purdy, *For Common Things: Irony, Trust, and Commitment in America Today* (New York: Alfred A. Knopf, 1999), 205-6.

52. Purdy, *Common Things,* 207.

53. Berlin, *Roots of Romanticism,* 109.

54. Purdy, *Common Things,* xxii.

55. Christina Nifong, "Cooperation Cuts a Community's Crime," *Christian Science Monitor* 89, no. 12 (11 December 1996): 1.

56. C. G. Jung, "Commentary," in *The Secret of the Golden Flower: A Chinese Book of Life* (New York: Harcourt, Brace & World, 1962), 85.

57. Wendell Berry, *What Are People For?: Essays* (San Francisco: North Point Press, 1990), 75-76.

58. Berry, *What Are People For?,* 85-86.

4

Civic Librarianship

This chapter will begin with a discussion of the contributions of the community movement perspective to professions that exercise social authority. The potential benefits of the community movement perspective to public librarianship will then be described. A working definition for civic librarianship will be provided and a series of reforms that this new perspective makes possible will be listed.

Contributions of the Community Movement Perspective to American Professions

The libertarian consensus advocates expressive and utilitarian individualism unbounded by social morality. One result of this perspective is the degradation of the work of professions. All professions propose to benefit society by helping to achieve some social purpose. Extreme individualism denies the legitimacy of social purposes and denies the social authority of those charged with carrying out these purposes.

Law enforcement personnel have been despised as enemies of the people. Teachers have been demoted to facilitators and co-learners. The public's reduced interest in citizenship has led to a decline in the role of journalists as protectors of the democracy. In each of these professions, people have been forced to reexamine the traditional work of their occupation in the light of a libertarian world without social purposes. The result of this examination has been an increasing reaffirmation of traditional social purposes using the ideas of the community movement. This new paradigm has had an especially powerful impact due to the success of collaborative techniques in contexts such as community policing.

The profession of journalism offers interesting parallels to the problems faced by librarians. The narrow economic goal of selling a media product has replaced the traditional role of a free press serving the democracy. The economic goal, which has been liberated from social purpose, has little to do with the journalistic goals of achieving accuracy, balancing coverage, and contributing to the democratic debate of public issues. The response of many journalists was to develop a "new" form of journalism that supported the traditional social goals of the professions in experimental new ways. E. J. Dionne Jr. considers the purposes of civic journalism.

> On the one hand, there is a need to resurrect a concern for what's true—to draw cleared distinctions between fact and opinion, between information and mere assertion, between flip predictions and reasoned analysis. At the same time, there is an urgent requirement that the media take seriously their obligation to draw people into the public debate, to demonstrate that the debate is accessible and that it matters. . . . What is needed, in other words, is both a strengthening of the older professional ethic involving accuracy and balance and a new engagement with the obligations of journalists to democracy.[1]

Critics of television journalism such as Newton Minow and Craig LaMay note that the public interest demands a higher level of accountability than journalists have generally wanted to accept. Minow and LaMay criticize the tendency among television journalists to avoid real accountability and to protect professional prerogatives by hiding behind the First Amendment. In their book *Abandoned in the Wasteland: Children, Television, and the First Amendment*, Minow and LaMay explain this problem.

> For half a century, anyone who has questioned the American commercial television system has been shouted down as a censor. Instead of talking seriously about how to improve television for our children, Americans argue to a stalemate about broadcasters' rights and government censorship. We neglect discussion of moral responsibility by converting the public interest into an economic abstraction, and we use the First Amendment to stop debate rather than to enhance it, thus reducing our first freedom to the logical equivalent of a suicide pact.

We have become accustomed to using the First Amendment to avoid asking ourselves hard questions which might require uncomfortable answers.[2]

Civic journalism seeks to develop positive social results through a rededication to the traditional moral purposes of the profession of journalism. This reform of journalism, although not as pervasive as community policing in law enforcement, gained strength throughout the 1990s. It has become increasingly obvious among journalists that both the self-respect of practitioners and the support of the public demand that journalists make a positive contribution to society.

A number of professions have used community movement ideas to reconstruct the social purpose and professional authority that has been lost in recent decades. Community movement ideas have also been used to develop powerful new ways to reach traditional professional goals in the context of contemporary society. Civic librarianship uses community movement ideas to achieve these important purposes in the institutional context of the public library.

Civic Librarianship

The following working definition of civic librarianship is offered to begin a dialogue among librarians and trustees concerning the use of community movement ideas in developing public libraries. *Civic librarianship seeks to strengthen communities through developmental strategies that renew the public library's mission of education for a democratic society.* Like civic journalism, civic librarianship reaffirms traditional professional values by using new strategies that address the needs of contemporary society.

Civic librarianship, as proposed here, affirms the traditional public library mission of education for a democratic society. Civic librarianship also, however, affirms the Public Library Inquiry's criticism that the traditional public library has often been ineffective in developing active, concrete strategies to accomplish this mission. Civic librarianship uses the strategies of the community movement to fulfill the mission of education for a democratic society.

The contrast between civic librarianship and the libertarian public library is striking. The libertarian public library features active, concrete strategies for achieving the goal of providing access to information for individuals. Marketing strategies for developing organizations that distribute materials and services have been extremely successful in the private sector. The problem with the libertarian public library is that public libraries are essentially community development and problem solving agencies, not distributors of materials and services. The distribution of materials and services has always been a means to achieve educational and community development results, not an end in itself.

As Douglas Raber has noted, the writers of the Public Library Inquiry understood that the great strength of the public library is that it is free of the demands of the marketplace.

> It is free from the economic rationality that demands that a product must find or create a sufficiently large enough audience to remain viable. In effect, the library is free to pursue its purpose in terms of the political rationality of needs rather than the market rationality of demands. Success can be measured in terms of the quality of and need for the product rather than the volume of use.[3]

When assessing the quality of materials and services is no longer important and assessing the importance of the need for these materials and services is no longer a concern, public librarianship is reduced to a technical, mechanical function that is no longer worthy of professional status. Responding to market demands can and should be done by less highly educated people, as is often the case in bookstores. Just as society does not need public librarians to achieve this simple purpose, it does not need the institution of the public library to pursue this non-educational goal. If the trustees of Boston Public Library had not proposed an educational mission for the public library, it is doubtful that their request for tax support would have been granted.

Although the writers of the Public Library Inquiry understood that the public library is not and should not be a market-driven institution, they nonetheless recommended a specific target market for the public library. Douglas Raber explains that these writers believed an "informed elite of active citizens" was the primary audience for the public library and that it was not an effective use of the institution's limited resources to attempt to provide a general community service.[4] This mistaken recommendation is a denial of the goal of universal participation in civic life and education that is the basic rationale for the institution.

Civic librarianship, then, affirms the worthy purpose of providing education for a democratic society and, in doing so, is strikingly different from the libertarian public library. Civic librarianship is also very different from the traditional public library, which has often failed to translate its mission into effective, concrete strategies for action. Civic librarianship proposes the active, concrete strategies of the community movement as a framework for achieving the traditional mission of education for a democratic society.

Several major tasks need to be accomplished by civic librarianship. These tasks include reestablishing the philosophical framework of public librarianship as well as developing strategies for action. The reforms of civic librarianship include the following:

- Restore the confidence of public librarians and trustees in exercising social authority.
- Renew the public library's historical mission of education for a democratic society.
- Develop the public library as a center of the community.
- Develop strategies to build communities through public library service.
- Use services and collections to meet social as well as individual needs.
- Strengthen the political efforts of public librarians and trustees.

Each of these tasks will be introduced in this chapter and addressed individually in succeeding chapters.

Restoring the Confidence of Public Librarians and Trustees in Exercising Social Authority

Society supports the lives of individuals in many critically important ways. In return for this help, it is reasonable for society to request the support of individuals for social purposes. Social authorities have the legal and moral right to carry out these social purposes. One of the most important social purposes in a democracy is public education. Public librarians and trustees have the legal and moral right to use the public library to fulfill the institution's democratic purpose of providing public education.

Unfortunately, expressive individualism has effectively challenged the legitimacy of social purposes and social authorities. The social purpose of education has been undercut not only by the general rejection of social purposes and social authority but also by the specific rejection of shared knowledge and social values as a basis for social order.

Community movement ideas support the general legitimacy of social purposes and authority as well as the particular importance of using rational knowledge and shared values in public education. The under-

standing of social authority and education that the community movement provides is vital to restoring the confidence of public librarians
and trustees in exercising their social authority.

Renewing the Public Library's Historical Mission of Education for a Democratic Society

The philosophy of the community movement gives public librarians
and trustees powerful support by demonstrating that knowledge is not
only useful but also vital to democratic decision making. The community movement supports the republican tradition of education that is the
philosophical foundation of the modern public library. In the republican
tradition, education is the basis for effective decision making and
viewed as essential to self-government. Education in this tradition
seeks to persuade and guide rather than to indoctrinate. Democratic
education communicates rational knowledge and shared social values
while honoring the individual's freedom to challenge these ideas and
values.

When public librarians and trustees accept the view that it is legitimate and useful to provide public education in a democracy, they reject
the challenges to the republican tradition presented by expressive individualism. The next step is to reject the alternative mission for the public library developed through the influence of utilitarian individualism.
Providing access to information for individuals is a weak social purpose. This is especially true in a society experiencing a surplus of information. It is critical to the future development of the public library
that the historical mission of providing education for a democratic society be renewed.

Developing the Public Library As a Center of the Community

Community movement literature is helpful in demonstrating the importance of the need for civic space. There is a critical need for places
that foster public dialogue and informal social interaction. This need
has been ignored in recent decades due to the extreme individualism of
American culture. The deterioration of local community life has increased the importance of those few institutions that continue to serve
communities as central points of coordination. The public library is one
such institution. Much can be done to increase the value of public libraries as centers of the community.

Developing the public library as a center of the community differs greatly from the developmental strategies of utilitarian individualism currently in vogue in public libraries. For example, treating library users as customers is now popular. This encourages the idea that users have the right to use the library, but no responsibilities for the use and development of the institution. This denies the responsibility of library users to become informed citizens and to support the funding of the library as an institution of public education. Library users are not customers; they are co-owners of a democratic institution that is shared by everyone.

Equally inappropriate is the strategy of developing the public library as a cluster of specialized market niches. It is the generalist nature of the public library that makes it valuable as a center of the community. The highly specialized and fragmented nature of the American society is a key reason why communities have deteriorated in recent decades. When public libraries reduce their appeal as places for everyone, they contribute to the problem, not the solution. A variety of other negative consequences of the indiscriminate use of marketing as a developmental strategy will be discussed in the chapter on this topic.

Developing Strategies to Build Communities through Public Library Service

Public libraries can help build communities by being places of community identity, community dialogue, community collaboration, and community evaluation. Community identity can be fostered by offering materials, services, and programs related to the history, natural environment, economy, government, organizations and social structures, culture and arts, and any other characteristics that might define the community. Civic dialogue can be encouraged by involving the library in activities that promote the institution as a public forum as well as a place for informal social interaction. Sponsoring lectures and discussions on public issues will promote civic dialogue as will simply providing meeting space for community groups. Social interaction can be encouraged through providing coffee and lounge areas of adequate size to meet this need. Public libraries can be focal points for organizing service agencies and groups to solve community problems. Public libraries can contribute the meeting space, information resources, and leadership to help organize effective responses to community needs. Public libraries can also serve as places for community evaluation where the strengths and weaknesses of the community can be analyzed.

Public libraries can help share planning documents and demographic studies from organizations throughout the community. Pooling the knowledge of community problems will contribute to the community's sense of identity, provide a factual basis for civic dialogue, and help develop priorities for problem solving through collaboration. Public libraries can also assist in community evaluation by working with other organizations and groups to develop more effective ways to assess the outcomes resulting from problem-solving efforts.

Utilizing Services and Collections to Meet Social As Well As Individual Needs

The ideology of the libertarian public library tends to view the institution as a quasi-retail operation that serves individuals in isolation from other organizations rather than as a community institution serving both individual and social needs as part of a network of social resources. The current bias against working with groups of people to provide library services arbitrarily limits a library's options for effective service. Ignoring the social context of individual life in choosing service options is bound to limit the impact of library services in meeting both social and individual needs. Developing library services in a social context necessarily includes working with groups and is therefore a political process. Success in developing political support for the library is based on providing effective service to groups as well as individuals.

Strengthening the Political Efforts of Public Librarians and Trustees

Public librarians and trustees are called upon to be advocates for the institution at the levels of local, state, and national community. This requires taking strong positions concerning the social benefits of public library service. Library leaders are reluctant, however, to take strong public positions due to a concern that people will lose faith in the neutrality and objectivity of the institution. This tension between advocacy and neutrality has caused a great deal of confusion among library leaders and has resulted in ineffective and dysfunctional political positions. Community movement ideas can help clarify the relationship between advocacy and neutrality.

Present-day library politics vacillates between the divisive, antisocial politics of expressive individualism and the social indifference of utilitarian individualism. The politics of expressive individualism often violates the principle of institutional neutrality; the politics of utilitarian individualism fails to advocate for the welfare of society. A unifying politics that advocates strongly for the essential values of the public library and also observes neutrality toward community groups needs to be developed.

Conclusion

The community movement offers society a positive, but realistic framework for strengthening America's endangered social structures. In reestablishing the validity of social purposes and the right of social authorities to carry out these purposes, community movement ideas have given new life and meaning to a wide range of professions that are required to exercise social authority. Public librarians and trustees can benefit from this general support for social authority as well as from the community movement's strong defense for public education as a requirement of democracy. The approach to public librarianship advocated here is an attempt to adapt community movement ideas as a means of both community and library reform.

Civic librarianship seeks to strengthen communities through developmental strategies that renew the public library's social mission of education for a democratic society. Like community policing and civic journalism, civic librarianship reaffirms traditional professional values by using new strategies that address the needs of contemporary society. Several major tasks need to be accomplished by civic librarianship. These tasks include the following:

- Restore the confidence of public librarians and trustees in exercising social authority.
- Renew the public library's historical mission of education for a democratic society.
- Develop the public library as a center of the community.
- Develop strategies to build communities through public library service.
- Utilize services and collections to meet social as well as individual needs.
- Strengthen the political efforts of public librarians and trustees by clarifying the relationship between advocacy and neutrality.

Civic librarianship reaffirms the traditional mission of the public library while providing new strategies for realizing this mission in a contemporary social context.

Jedediah Purdy begins his book *For Common Things: Irony, Trust, and Commitment in America Today* with a very telling quote from Czeslaw Milosz, "'What is unpronounced tends to nonexistence.'"[5] If public librarians and trustees no longer speak for the older tradition, the finest aspects of the public library and its relationship with the public will be gradually lost. Library leaders need to learn again how to speak the language of the great tradition of the public library. They need to translate this language into a contemporary world that is often antagonistic to the purposes of public education and democracy itself. Community movement ideas can help library leaders to renew the moral and intellectual framework necessary for public librarianship to continue its historic contribution to the life of the nation.

Notes

1. E. J. Dionne Jr., *They Only Look Dead: Why Progressives Will Dominate the Next Political Era* (New York: Simon & Schuster, 1996), 254.

2. Newton N. Minow and Craig L. LaMay, *Abandoned in the Wasteland: Children, Television, and the First Amendment* (New York: Hill and Wang, 1995), 6.

3. Douglas Raber, *Librarianship and Legitimacy: The Ideology of the Public Library Inquiry* (Westport, Conn.: Greenwood Press, 1997), 94.

4. Raber, *Librarianship and Legitimacy*, 97.

5. Jedediah Purdy, *For Common Things: Irony, Trust, and Commitment in America Today* (New York: Alfred A. Knopf, 1999), [ix].

5

Restoring Democratic Social Authority

The libertarian consensus of the 1980s grew out of the expressive individualism of the political Left and the utilitarian individualism of the political Right. This consensus, which continued to influence the politics of the 1990s, seeks to base our national life almost entirely on the preservation of individual liberty. The other pillar of American life, which Oliver Garceau called "the democratic process of group life,"[1] is acknowledged only to the extent that the democratic process supports individual rights. Education and other attempts to socialize individuals are viewed as affronts to personal liberty. The community movement renews respect for the social context of individual life and reminds the nation that no society can perpetuate itself without deliberate and effective efforts to teach individuals the knowledge and values upon which their society is based.

The libertarian consensus of the 1980s had a profound effect upon the public library. In keeping with the views of expressive individualism, the libertarian public library challenges both the validity of rational knowledge and society's right to influence the individual. As a result of these challenges, the public library abandoned its mission to provide education for a democratic society and replaced it with the mission of providing access to information for individuals. The new mission owes its substance and developmental strategies to the utilitarian individualism of the marketplace. In this chapter, community movement ideas will be used to respond to the challenge presented by expressive individualism to the social authority of public librarians and trustees. The chapter will begin with a description of current problems in exercising social authority, which will be followed by a defense of the appropriate exercise of social authority.

Problems in Exercising Social Authority

The most basic task of civic librarianship is to restore the confidence of public librarians and trustees in the exercise of social authority. As the libertarian perspective of the 1980s has supported individuals to the detriment of social purposes, social authority has lost much of its power. The tradition of expressive individualism has been harsh in its denunciation of the use of social authority. In the heyday of the counterculture, social authorities of all types were stigmatized. Law enforcement officials, who drew some of the most abusive treatment, were commonly referred to as "pigs."

Public librarians and trustees are legally appointed to serve as social authorities, but not given the full moral authority to do this work. In response to this awkward situation, librarians and trustees have tried to develop ways to educate without educating and lead without leading. Although these efforts have a certain mystical appeal, their self-contradictory nature is problematic. The conflict inherent in being authority figures who do not believe in social authority results in a debilitating timidity in exercising authority.

Public librarians and trustees are social authorities appointed to share their knowledge with their communities. In addition to this educational authority, library administrators and trustees are given the authority to manage library personnel, finances, and facilities. Some administrators and trustees are also given the authority to represent their libraries as community, state, and national leaders. Each of these types of authority is an important responsibility. If public librarians and trustees do not believe that it is legitimate to exercise social authority, they will be deeply conflicted about the work they are appointed to do and unlikely to perform these duties well.

Educational Authority

As selectors of materials and services, public librarians often express a relativism that makes them appear to be unable to make the most routine judgments about the world. For example, many librarians cannot bring themselves to confidently describe as harmful any type of materials or services. In a 1999 article in *American Libraries*, American Library Association Intellectual Freedom Committee member Carrie Gardner responds to the question "Can we agree that there are materials that are harmful to minors?" in this manner.[2]

> The question was, can we all agree that there are materials harmful to minors? I think that that phrase, that idea, has become a catch-all for a lot of ideas, images, and information on the Internet that makes people uncomfortable. And so one thing that a lot of folks have done is say, "Oh, that's harmful to minors, that's harmful to our children," when, in fact, there is no research saying that it's harmful.[3]

Although this response is intended to be a strong defense of intellectual freedom, it demonstrates both an alarming lack of interest in the educational impact of library services and an extreme timidity in the exercise of social authority required to select materials and services.

Administrative Authority

A similar timidity is evident in the area of administrative authority over library finances, personnel, and facilities. Examples of this timidity can be found in prevalent attitudes toward enforcing rules for library use and supervising library staff. Rules for library use are often viewed as obstacles to public service that place illegitimate constraints on the individual rather than as necessary expressions of social authority that ensure good service. Popular "customer service" workshops for librarians have helped to dilute the impact of patron rules by encouraging an extreme inability to "say no" to those using the library. The existence of rules for library use is viewed as a necessary evil or, worse yet, as an evil that can and should be overridden in cases of controversy by the primacy of individual rights. These rules are rarely described as positive social safeguards designed to support fair and effective service. If rules for library use were viewed as necessary aspects of the institution's social authority, they might be seen as offering an opportunity to educate the public to the merits of the public library as a service institution rather than as embarrassing transgressions against individual liberty.

A similar evasion of the duties of social authority is found in extreme forms of antihierarchical personnel management. Flat organizational structures, for whatever other value they might have, often appeal to administrators who do not believe in the exercise of social authority required in traditional supervision. Many library administrators do not want to be a "boss" because they do not believe that this function is either necessary or morally justifiable. If the exercise of authority is essential to social life, it follows that it is ill advised to develop structures that go beyond encouraging staff participation toward the abdication of supervisory responsibility. Much more common than the development of such dysfunctional new organizational structures is the simple abdication of supervision within traditional structures. Although library administrators often view such loose supervisory practices as high-minded, such practices are, in the final analysis, a refusal to do the work for which the supervisor is hired.

Library Leadership

The acceptance and exercise of social authority is most important for public libraries at the level of community, state, and national leadership. Timidity in this area is extremely damaging to the social and political health of the institution. Efforts in recent years to promote advocacy for public libraries have been confronted with the fact that librarians are, by ideology, extremely reluctant to tell others what to do. As Patricia Glass Schuman writes in a 1999 article in *American Libraries*, "Yet there are some who consider speaking up for libraries to be 'unseemly'—even dangerous—because they associate library advocacy with taking a stand for a particular point of view, or representing a special interest."[4] This reluctance to take a position in support of the most basic values of the institution may be more damaging to the development of leadership among public librarians and trustees than any other single factor. A person cannot lead without taking a position and forcefully making a case for that position. It is understandable, of course, that people are reluctant to establish themselves as leaders at a time when the general culture is so hostile to leadership. It would seem that the safer approach would be to quietly follow the will of the community as suggested in *A Planning Process for Public Libraries* and its successors. The safety of this approach, however, is purchased at the expense of the institution's future. The public library cannot succeed if library leaders will not fight for it.

Abdicating leadership roles, for whatever reason, will result in the decline of the institution. This weakness is especially unnecessary as there is a great deal of advice available to help public librarians and trustees become effective leaders in public education. Prominent examples include the advocacy materials and workshops offered by the American Library Association and the Benton Foundation's handbook *The Future's in the Balance: A Toolkit for Libraries and Communities in the Digital Age.* No amount of good advice will help, however, if public librarians and trustees are unwilling to accept the responsibility to stand up for the public library as an institution dedicated to the mission of education for a democratic society.

Public librarians and trustees are required by tradition and by law to function as social authorities in their educational roles, in their administrative capacities, and in their leadership roles in the larger communities to which libraries belong. In recent decades, however, public librarians, trustees, and many other Americans have lost the understanding of and respect for the proper role of social authority in a democracy. It is time to regain this understanding and respect. The literature and perspective of the community movement can help reconstruct a healthier, more positive view of the work of social authorities. Without such an understanding of social authority, public librarians and trustees simply cannot perform their duties with the confidence and intensity that these jobs require.

Restoring the Confidence of Library Leaders in Exercising Social Authority

The authority of public librarians and trustees is derived from two sources. A natural authority is derived from the fact that library leaders have obtained certain types of knowledge that society requires. To extend the benefits of this knowledge to other citizens, society has granted public librarians and trustees the legal authority to share this knowledge with others. Expressive individualism, as noted earlier, challenges both the authority of knowledge and society's authority to educate the individual. The community movement responds to this position by defending the value of knowledge and by demonstrating that the effective exercise of social authority in public education is critical to the success of the democracy.

Defending Knowledge in the Context of Democratic Decision Making

The intellectual and moral relativism of the libertarian public library is, in part, the descendent of Romanticism's original attack on the Enlightenment's confidence in rational knowledge. To promote individual freedom, expressive individualism rejects rational knowledge and moral values that can be shared by a society in favor of the subjectivity of individual emotion and instinct. The strength of the individual will to mold reality is the measure of success. Even behavior that is considered to be extremely irrational or immoral by social standards, such as the behavior described by the Marquis De Sade, is viewed favorably in the sense that it is a triumph of the individual will over social conformity. This rejection of a social reality governed by rationality and shared moral values is a distortion of the human condition because it denies the social nature of human life. As Isaiah Berlin noted, the perspective of Romanticism is "fallacious" to the extent that "human beings, in order to communicate with each other, are forced to recognize certain common values, certain common facts, to live in a common world."[5]

A major contribution of the community movement has been to powerfully delineate how the individual is related to the common life provided by American democracy. Writers such as James Q. Wilson and Amitai Etzioni have made a strong case for the position that the intellectual and moral relativism of expressive individualism is both untrue to the human condition and socially destructive. Community movement writers explain that rational knowledge and shared moral values are critically important to democratic decision making and social cohesion.

This view of knowledge and morality in a democratic society resonates with the initial philosophical justification for supporting the public library through taxation. The original trustees of Boston Public Library wrote that, "the largest number of persons should be induced to read and understand questions going down to the very foundations of social order, which are constantly presenting themselves, and which we, as a people, are constantly required to decide, and do decide, either ignorantly or wisely."[6]

Support for the social usefulness of knowledge was powerfully reaffirmed by the Public Library Inquiry one hundred years later. The community movement assists public librarians and trustees by reminding them of the continued power of this great tradition.

If rational knowledge and shared social values are useful, the public library is useful. The community movement can help public librarians and trustees to renew their confidence in the ability of knowledge and shared values to improve society. It has traditionally been the job of public librarians and trustees to help people find and effectively use the best available knowledge to improve both individual and social life. The work of public librarians and trustees cannot make sense without the confidence that this work can and should be done.

Defending Society's Right to Influence Individuals

The community movement supports the idea that there must be a balance between individual rights and the individual's responsibilities to society. The individual benefits greatly from social support and is morally bound to help maintain society. Institutions and authority figures of various types are needed to educate individuals to accept their responsibilities and, when necessary, to enforce the acceptance of these responsibilities. This encouragement and enforcement, according to the community movement, must take place in a democratic context respectful of individual autonomy.

At first glance, the community movement's position on social authority would appear to be unobjectionable. The culture war has shown us, however, that the social conservatives of the Right and the expressive individualists of the Left both disagree with this approach to social authority. Social conservatives have shown great enthusiasm for the exercise of social authority as a means of controlling human nature, which they view as essentially evil. This enthusiasm has, no doubt, helped to fuel the massive development of prisons in the 1990s. Expressive individualists, on the other hand, accept the Romantic position that any use of social authority is oppressively authoritarian. In the general culture, this view has contributed to replacing the extreme reverence for authority figures common in the 1950s with an equally inappropriate hatred and mistrust for authority figures in our current culture. The false choice between oppressive social authority that does not respect individual autonomy and the wholesale rejection of social authority has helped to fuel the cultural civil war.

The community movement offers a middle-ground position, a balance between individual liberty and social order. Being a social authority in a democracy requires a person to balance individual autonomy and the welfare of society in an institutional context, just as the democracy is itself designed to achieve such a balance. The choice is no longer between abdication of authority and authoritarianism. The literature of the community movement offers instruction in the lost art of exercising social authority in a democratic context. Before public libraries can effectively pursue the mission of education for a democratic society, the confidence of public librarians and trustees in the authority of society to influence individuals must be reestablished. Community movement ideas can be useful in achieving this important goal.

Exercising Democratic Social Authority

The cultural war has offered two leadership options, authoritarian leadership or the abdication of leadership. Neither of these forms of leadership is appropriate to a democratic society. Dictatorship has never been popular in America and the counterculture's abdication of leadership has proven to be a disaster. A democracy balances the rights of the individual with the needs of the society. Leaders in a democracy are responsible for organizing this balancing act. This makes sense, but is also very troublesome. It is easier to try to control everything or to meekly follow the will of the people than it is to make decisions in an atmosphere of social participation. The hard work of democracy, however, requires this course of action. It is the only course of action that can succeed in today's world.

Amitai Etzioni's idea that a good society must have a high level of both individual rights and responsibilities is valuable in demonstrating how organizational leadership can be improved.[7] Leaders today must be stronger in encouraging broad social participation in decision making. They must also be more assertive in using their own knowledge and expertise to make and implement decisions when the process of consulting with staff members and constituents has been completed. In public libraries, everyone has the right and the responsibility to contribute to decision making. Library leaders have the right and the responsibility to make decisions as well as the right and responsibility to solicit social participation in the process.

Another way to think about the complex process of democratic leadership is offered by the discipline of systems analysis, which is the basis for most types of long-range planning. Before designing a new system, the existing system must be understood. Studying the existing system includes studying the environment in which the system exists as well as the internal workings of the system. In systems analysis, every system serves a larger system. Public libraries, for example, serve their communities. Once the internal workings and the needs of the larger system are understood, the design of a new and improved organization can begin. The implementation of the new design is intended to result in improved service to the larger system.

In the discipline of systems analysis, two very different types of thinking are required. When studying the larger environment, *open systems* thinking is needed. People need to be open to the larger environment in all of its complexity. The open systems perspective requires holistic, right brain thinking and great sensitivity. This perspective is challenging because it permits the consideration of changes that leaders may fear. In public library planning, for example, careful listening to staff members and constituents requires openness and courage.

The design of the new system requires the analytical, left brain work of *closed system* thinking. This is the stage at which leaders must choose from all they have observed in the open phase. This requires the design of a new structure for the policies, procedures, staffing, technology, facilities, and so forth that are to be changed. This is the stage that requires leaders to stop listening and make difficult decisions.

The example of public library planning can be used to demonstrate the two basic ways to fail in the process of developing a new system. First, the open phase of the process can fail to adequately determine the needs of the larger system. If public library leaders misunderstand community needs, it will be impossible for them to effectively redesign the organization to meet these needs. This failure is most likely to occur when leaders do not listen to those around them. Second, even when community needs are properly understood, the closed phase of the process can fail to develop an effective institutional design to meet these needs.

Authoritarian leadership fails by neglecting open systems thinking; the non-leadership of expressive individualism fails by neglecting closed system thinking. Democracy requires that leaders are both open to social participation and effective in using the perspective they gain from listening to make decisions. Democratic leadership is, at its deepest level, the art of integrating and balancing individual and social needs and identities. This complex balancing act, which is rejected by both authoritarians and expressive individualists, is described by Jean Lipman-Blumen in her book *Connective Leadership: Managing in a Changing World*, in which she says,

> the overarching task of leadership is to help us connect these two dialectics between self and Other, one functioning at the individual level and the other at the societal level. If we can connect the societal dialectic between diversity (focused on individual identity) and interdependence (emphasizing the collective Other) to our individual developmental dialectic (between self and Other), we will finally understand the complex meanings of life to which our personal developmental dialectic has been dedicated.[8]

Conclusion

It is possible for public librarians and trustees to succeed as democratic social authorities. Library leaders have natural authority because they have the knowledge that society needs to function as a democracy. They also have the legal authority to share this knowledge with the community. Leadership in a democratic institution such as the public library cannot be authoritarian and must show respect for individual rights. It is equally inappropriate for library leaders to adopt the anti-leadership style of expressive individualism. Democratic leadership is the complex art of balancing individual and social needs. The ideas of the community movement provide a strategy for regaining a balanced, democratic approach to leadership. If public librarians and trustees accept the usefulness of knowledge and the right of society to educate the individual, they can restore both their own confidence and society's confidence in the social authority of the institution.

Notes

1. Oliver Garceau et al., *The Public Library in the Political Process* (Boston: Gregg Press, 1972), 144.

2. "Children's Access: Protection or Preparation?" *American Libraries* 30, no.10 (November 1999): 59-60.

3. "Children's Access," 59.

4. Patricia Glass Schuman, "Speaking Up and Speaking Out: Ensuring Equity through Advocacy," *American Libraries* 30, no. 9 (October 1999): 50.

5. Isaiah Berlin, *The Roots of Romanticism* (Princeton: Princeton University Press, 1999), 146.

6. Jesse H. Shera, *Foundations of the Public Library: Origins of the Public Library Movement in New England 1629-1855* (Chicago: University of Chicago Press, 1949; n.p.: Shoe String Press, 1965), 281.

7. Amitai Etzioni, *The New Golden Rule: Community and Morality in a Democratic Society* (New York: Basic Books, 1996), 42.

8. Jean Lipman-Blumen, *Connective Leadership: Managing in a Changing World* (Oxford: Oxford University Press, 1996), 331.

6

Renewing the Educational Mission

In addition to reestablishing the social authority of public librarians and trustees to influence individuals, the community movement provides support for reestablishing education for a democratic society as the mission of the public library. In a powerful restatement of the republican tradition, the community movement reminds people of the critical need for public education in a democracy. If it is true, as the republican tradition maintains, that human nature is a mixture of good and evil, decision making is important. The success of democracy requires that self-governing citizens make intellectually sound decisions in the context of shared social values. Education is the essential preparation for democratic decision making. Providing education to support people in making decisions is the rationale for the modern public library.

With the exception of the republican tradition, the major strands of American culture do not offer a strong a framework for public education and public library service. The biblical tradition, in the extreme form of the Puritanism of the Religious Right, appears to want education to be indoctrination into a theocracy. The expressive individualism of Romanticism challenges both the validity of knowledge and society's right to influence the individual through education or any other means. The tradition of utilitarian individualism treats education, not as preparation for the duties of citizenship but rather as a tool for personal economic advancement.

The traditional public library mission of education for a democratic society is derived from the republican tradition. The libertarian public library's mission of access to information for individuals is derived from the traditions of expressive and utilitarian individualism. Before the public library is completely redrawn according to the libertarian mission, public librarians and trustees need to examine the serious limitations of this new public library mission.

The libertarian public library is limited by both the antisocial and antieducational values of expressive individualism and by inappropriate goals and developmental methods acquired from utilitarian individualism. Expressive individualism negates the mission of education for a democratic society by denying the validity of both rational knowledge and social authority. Once the traditional mission has been repudiated, the utilitarian mission of providing access to information for individuals wins by default. The utilitarian mission brings with it the cultural values and the developmental strategies of the marketplace.

The previous chapter on the social authority of public librarians and trustees responded to the challenge expressive individualism has presented to the educational mission of the public library. In this section, the challenge of the other ideological tradition supporting the libertarian public library, the tradition of utilitarian individualism, will be addressed. The utilitarian individualism of the private sector filled the void created by the defeat of social purposes such as education. Rather than to further describe the importance of public education in community movement literature, this section will explore the viability of the libertarian public library's mission of access to information for individuals as a replacement for the public library's traditional mission of education for a democratic society. This section will begin with the Public Library Inquiry's critique of the idea of a noneducational, demand-oriented public library based on utilitarian individualism. The discussion of the theoretical and practical limitations of this approach to public library development will next be brought up to date with discussions of Neil Postman's book *The End of Education: Redefining the Value of School* and David Schenk's book *Data Smog: Surviving the Information Glut.*

The Public Library Inquiry Views
Utilitarian Individualism As a Basis
for the Public Library Mission

The Public Library Inquiry found that, although most librarians supported the serious agenda of social education reflected in the consolidated list of 1940s objectives in chapter 3, other librarians preferred an approach to public library development similar to today's libertarian public library. Robert Leigh's critique of a noneducational, demand-oriented public library is full of meaning for today's library leaders.

> There was in our sample a small but energetic minority who see the public library's task solely as "giving people what they want," who supply books, good or bad, on the basis of expressed public demand irrespective of quality, reliability, or value. To them public libraries are a free, miscellaneous book service supported by the public for that purpose rather than a governmental service of reliable information and continuous education as implied in the objectives approved by the majority of librarians.
>
> This alternative not only turns away abruptly from the librarian's traditional faith in the ameliorative power of books, but also engages the public library in direct competition with the commercial agencies of communication on their own terms. As a long-term goal, it would assign to the public library a supplementary and secondary rather than distinctive role in the whole communication field, or would doom it to gradual extinction because of the greater resources, reach, and competitive skill of the commercial media of mass communication.
>
> To have applied the alternative objective to present library practice and program would mean setting up the standards of mass production, distribution, and consumption as public library goals. To meet such standards would lead logically to central purchase of uniformly popular books and periodicals, and no others, to many small and large outlets dealing almost entirely with current publications manned by persons selected for qualities of salesmanship rather than scholarship, to results judged entirely in terms of volume of circulation and numbers of users.[1]

The utilitarian individualism underlying this alternate mission for the public library is alive and well in the libertarian public library. Once the educational mission of the public library is gone, the public library will have no distinctive service to offer. Duplicating the services of commercial entities will place the public library in a weakened and decidedly subordinate position. This direct competition with the private sector will not be successful due to the public library's lack of resources. The end result could well be the extinction of the institution. One of the

most obvious results of this change of mission is Leigh's observation
that salesmanship will replace scholarship. The higher level of education required for librarianship is directly tied to the educational mission.
Society does not need and will not pay for people with masters degrees
to manage a materials distribution service. The private-sector techniques used to develop such a service cannot succeed because the mission of the libertarian public library cannot succeed.

Public Education and the Need
for a Purposeful Narrative

In his book *The End of Education: Redefining the Value of School*, Neil
Postman explains that public education is no longer inspired by a com-
pelling purpose or end and that this lack of purpose threatens to end
public education. He says that

> in America, as elsewhere, there exists what Vaclav Havel calls "a crisis in
> narrative." Old gods have fallen, either wounded or dead. New ones have
> been aborted. "We are looking," he said, "for new scientific recipes, new
> ideologies, new control systems, new institutions. . . . " In other words,
> we seek new gods who can provide us with "an elementary sense of jus-
> tice, the ability to see things as others do, a sense of transcendental re-
> sponsibility, archetypal wisdom, good taste, courage, compassion, and
> faith."[2]

Postman is greatly concerned by Western culture's inability to find
meaning and the crippling effect this has had on social institutions.

> It is difficult to say if this erosion of symbols, this obliteration of the
> difference between the sacred and the profane, is the effect or the cause
> of a crisis in narrative. . . . Whichever the case, we are led to conclude
> that it is not a good time for gods and their symbols, and is therefore a
> bad time for social institutions that draw their power from metaphysical
> sources.[3]

Barring the renewal of great themes such as education for a democracy or the creation of powerful new narratives, Postman predicts that
public education as currently known may end. He notes that

> the end of public schooling—"end" meaning its conversion to privatized
> schooling (as Henry Perkinson predicts in his updated version of *The Im-
> perfect Panacea*) or its subordination to individually controlled technol-

ogy (as Lewis Perelman predicts in *School's Out.*) It is also possible that schooling will be taken over by corporations (as, for example, in the way Chris Whittle proposes) and operated entirely on principles associated with a market economy.[3]

Postman's book reminds readers that it is not enough to choose a mission and to use effective techniques to market this mission. The intrinsic value of the chosen mission is critically important. If the mission is lacking in purposefulness, it may well be that it is impossible to sell. Only the most purposeful missions receive local tax support in the United States. Both expressive individualism and utilitarian individualism encourage public librarians and trustees to believe that the selection of public library mission is bounded only by the limits of creativity and marketing skill. In fact, the selection of mission is limited by the extreme social requirements that any mission must meet before receiving tax support.

As public librarians move from providing education to providing access, they move from the high professional calling of improving people's lives to the technical, mechanical process of distributing materials and services without regard for the impact these materials and services might have on people's lives. When the profession of public librarianship is defined in a technical, mechanical way, it should not surprise librarians when people assume that they are technicians. When services are presented without regard for the impact of these services on the health of the individual or the society as a whole, it should not surprise librarians that people do not find the work of librarians to be inspiring in terms of moral purpose.

Education for a democratic society is the great narrative behind the public library as an institution. The selection of this mission was an act of genius that resulted in a powerful national movement. This narrative can still inspire. Although the public is not fully aware of the non-educational mission of the libertarian public library, challenges to this mission will increase as public awareness increases. The continued support of the mission of access to information for individuals threatens the viability of the public library as a national institution.

The Declining Need for Access to Information

The new mission of providing access to information for individuals fails to inspire support not only because it disregards the human result of the work of public libraries but also because simple access to information is no longer society's basic problem. As David Shenk notes in his book *Data Smog: Surviving the Information Glut*, "Information, once rare and cherished like caviar, is now plentiful and taken for granted like potatoes."[4]

> Just as fat has replaced starvation as this nation's number one dietary concern, information overload has replaced information scarcity as an important new emotional, social, and political problem. "The real issue for future technology," says Columbia's Eli Noam, "does not appear to be production of information, and certainly not transmission. Almost anybody can *add* information. The difficult question is how to *reduce* it.[5]

Shenk explains that although we need less information, we need more education. He says,

> embrace the joys of education as the best possible antidote to data smog. Education . . . is anti-glut. It is the harnessing of information, organizing it into knowledge and memory. Education also breeds a healthy skepticism, and will help consumers fend off manipulative marketing tactics. Education is the one thing we can't get overloaded with. The more of it the better.[6]

Access has never been a less convincing rationale for the public library. Contrasted to the lack of need for access is an increased need for education to help people sort through the vast glut of information. An additional practical problem related to the access mission is that the public library faces tremendous competition from a vast array of commercial interests that have grown considerably in recent years. As usual, the more time-intensive and complex task of education is left largely to those who do not seek a profit. Education is a high professional calling that is morally purposeful. Education is desperately needed by our society. Access is a mechanical function that is relatively easy to provide and generally taken for granted in our information-rich society. Both society's needs and the need for public libraries to continue to receive tax support argue for an educational mission.

Conclusion

From the report of the Boston trustees in 1852 and throughout the history of the public library, the moral purpose of improving the democracy through the provision of education has been the rationale for the existence of the public library. A Gallup poll taken in 1992 confirmed that the American public continues to view the public library as an educational institution.[7] Support for the public library is based on this perception.

This is so despite the willingness of public librarians and trustees to accept the civil libertarian view that the public library provides access, not education. This view is demonstrated by the Jenner and Block law firm's recent memorandum to the American Library Association that proclaims that "the primary library mission" is "providing access to a broad and diverse range of materials."[8] The public believes that education is the public library's primary mission; the dominant ideology of librarianship supports the provision of access as the public library's primary mission. Although this tension has existed for decades, the recent discussion of Internet filtering in public libraries has begun to inform the general public of the new access mission that has been pursued without their knowledge or authorization.

Regardless of the resolution of the Internet filtering controversy, the public library will be damaged by the strident proclamations of library associations and individuals that the public library is not overtly educational, but simply a provider of access. Providing a materials distribution service without a positive social purpose is not a sufficient basis for the institution to justify public support. Patrick Williams concludes his book *The Public Library and the Problem of Purpose* with the following words.

> There is no question of the value of restoring the library to its educational task. Education does not need to prove its value. Education is what the library can provide. Education is what the public wants from the library. The time is ripe for restoration. . . . The history of the public library argues that restoration is the only course that is worthy, the only course that leads anywhere. The American public has always wanted and still wants the public library to be an educational institution. And, in all probability, the public will not have it otherwise.[9]

Neil Postman's concerns that public education may come to an end need to be taken seriously. As an institution of public education, the public library's fate is inextricably bound with the fate of the public school. The public library is in real danger of being privatized, displaced by individually controlled technologies, or displaced by bookstores. This is true not because the private sector will compete for the public library's mission of education for a democratic society, but because public librarians and trustees are abandoning this mission. In making the mission of the public library indistinguishable from private sector entities, public librarians and trustees make the public library unnecessary.

Notes

1. Robert D. Leigh, *The Public Library in the United States* (New York: Columbia University Press, 1950), 224.
2. Neil Postman, *The End of Education: Redefining the Value of School* (New York: Vintage Books, 1995), 23-24.
3. Postman, *End of Education*, 25-26.
4. Postman, *End of Education*, 61.
5. David Shenk, *Data Smog: Surviving the Information Glut* (New York: HarperEdge, 1997), 27.
6. Shenk, *Data Smog*, 202-3.
7. George D'Elia and Eleanor Jo Rodger, "Public Opinion about the Roles of the Public Library in the Community: The Results of a Recent Gallup Poll," *Public Libraries* (January/February 1994), 23-28.
8. Jenner and Block, "Internet Filtering in Public Libraries," Memorandum to American Library Association 2000, http://www.ftrf.org/internetfiltering memo.html (4 February 2000).
9. Patrick Williams, *The American Public Library and the Problem of Purpose* (New York: Greenwood Press, 1988), 137.

7

A Center of the Community

A third major task for civic librarianship is to explore the public library's potential to serve as a center of the community. One of the most powerful insights that can be gained from the community movement is that communities are in desperate need of the civic space necessary for community building. Although the community movement has tended to overlook the role of the public library as a civic space, both the present reality and the future potential of this function for libraries is impressive. To take advantage of the great potential for public libraries to serve as centers for their communities, public librarians and trustees will need a fuller understanding of their opportunities for this service. They will also need to be willing to take a more active role in the leadership of their communities. This chapter will discuss the potential for the public library to expand its role as a center of the community and explain how the concept of functioning as a center of the community could serve as a developmental model for the institution. In discussing this model, the strategy of developing the public library as a center of the community will be shown to be strikingly different from the underlying philosophy of popular private-sector developmental strategies such as customer service training and market niche development.

The Potential for an Expanded Role

Public libraries are naturally positioned at the center of their communities because they serve everyone in an open and accessible manner. Public library buildings are often at the geographic center of their communities, often feature evening and weekend hours of operation, and are generally physically accessible to those with disabilities. People of all ages, races, socioeconomic backgrounds, and interests meet together in public libraries. Most public libraries have meeting rooms that are used by a wide variety of community groups. Public libraries are a primary source of information on local history and culture and present special programs on these topics. Public libraries work with other organizations to celebrate and improve local community life.

The potential for an increased public library role in community building is now being actively discussed in books such as *A Place at the Table: Participating in Community Building* by Kathleen de la Peña McCook and *Civic Space/Cyberspace: The American Public Library in the Information Age* by Redmond Kathleen Molz and Phyllis Dain. Molz and Dain point to a new stress on the civic role of the public library.

> Clearly the evidence points to the public library as having utilitarian and educational value to people and to communities. But its social significance runs deeper. It is a material symbol of civic culture and of society's cultural heritage. Public libraries are free, open, voluntary, neutral territory, and they do have something for everyone, from cradle to grave. They exemplify democratic freedoms and the American belief in the right to knowledge. In a library people are surrounded by human history—by the achievements, and failures, of human civilization. People need and want this environment and the sense of identity it sustains. . . .
>
> Libraries' unique characteristics take on special meaning today, when thoughtful people worry about the fragmentation of contemporary life and the apparent decline of local activities that bound people together in the past. The work of social scientists like Robert N. Bellah and Robert Putnam on the value of communities, civic institutions, and participation in public life, of Amitai Etzioni and the new communitarianism, of Withold Rybczynski on the vitality of urban life, of Tony Hiss on *The Experience of Place* and Ray Oldenburg on *Great Good Places* has focused interest on civic culture and along with it, civic space. We see new attention given to the meaning of *place*, to social interaction, not in anonymous commercial suburban malls or in chatting at home with computer buddies in the new communities of cyberspace, but in neighborhood institutions in real space. People are looking for social moorings. Libraries—stable, welcoming, venerable, but also modern—make good

candidates. They are associated with education and culture and understood as communal property but not too associated with government.
Although public opinion surveys do not rank the library as a formal
meeting place as highly as other roles, community groups do use library
meeting rooms (quite heavily in the libraries we visited), and library programs do attract audiences (by the tens and hundreds of thousands annu-
ally in large cities and counties). Current social comment often couples
the renewal of civic culture with the need to revive civility and to offset
the vulgarity and crass commercialism of much of American life. Libraries, of course, are classically civilized places (although not quite as
hushed as they used to be).[1]

William Fulton, chair of the Library Advisory Commission for the
City of Ventura, California, wrote in 1998 that institutions like public
libraries will be increasingly important as centers of their communities.
"Today, these civic institutions—libraries, performing-arts centers,
schools, farmers' markets, youth-sports leagues, service clubs—are on
the rise again. They hold the potential to be new glue of U.S. towns by
drawing people back into community life."[2] He is especially enthusias-
tic about the role libraries may play in this important work.

Libraries offer the best example. No civic institution has been thrown
more deeply into crisis by the financial and technological changes of the
last 20 years. . . .
   Many libraries are rising to the challenge by transforming themselves
into places where townspeople go not just to read but to do. The successful library is a parade of people, activities, programs, attractions—a collection of events that draws people away from their televisions and com-
puters and, by doing so, helps them restore the sense of community identity that has been missing ever since the local bank or the local department store got swallowed by a chain.[3]

The civic role of libraries has been celebrated by two consecutive
presidents of the American Library Association. Sarah Ann Long's
choice of "Libraries Build Community" as the theme for her 1999-2000
presidential year and Nancy Kranich's 2000-2001 theme "Libraries:
The Cornerstone of Democracy" have greatly advanced this discussion.
Experiments in community building through library service are now
being recognized by the national media. A recent article in the *New
York Times* cited one such effort at the Queens Borough Public Library.
Dean E. Murphy writes that,

The approach has put Queens at the forefront of a major shift at public libraries across the country away from strictly scholarly pursuits toward

functions once associated with community centers, religious and business organizations, the Y.M.C.A. and even small colleges. As libraries undergo extensive changes to cope with competition with mega-bookstores, the Internet and the digital age, they are finding ways to become more essential in the neighborhoods that surround them.[4]

An important dialogue is underway that promises to help librarians in all settings discover powerful new social dimensions for library service that resonate with the best traditions of the profession.

Public librarians and trustees are beginning to realize that the increasingly fragmented and specialized nature of American society has encouraged the freedom of specific groups and individuals while neglecting the maintenance of common social structures, one of which is the public library itself. The resulting loss of community connections and coordination has been extremely damaging. Dysfunction at the level of families, neighborhoods, and communities has seriously threatened the stability and sustainability of our culture. The community movement has called for an environmental movement to protect and strengthen these social structures. Public libraries can play an important role in this effort.

Before describing how public libraries can protect and strengthen their communities, it should be first noted that the public library is *a* center of the community, not *the* center of the community. Although the public library, as a central and neutral institution, is well positioned to help in this process, it is not suggested here that the public library is or ought to be *the* center of the community. When the complex webs of relationships that constitute our communities are analyzed, it is clear that the public library is only one of a number of important organizations that serves as a focal point of community life. The relative strength of the public library among these focal points will vary from community to community. Although librarians and trustees can maximize the strength of their organizations by fully utilizing the natural advantages of the public library as a center of community, the goal here is to improve service, not to find an edge in competing with other organizations. The stronger the other centers of community are, the less need there will be for the public library to provide this type of service. The goal here is not to carve out new power for the public library, but to help strengthen communities where this needs to be done.

The public library does not need to be *the* center of the community to make a significant contribution in providing civic space for community development. The public library is one of the few common social structures in local communities that are increasingly served by public-

and private-sector entities organized at the state, national, or global level, but disconnected from each other at the level of the local community. The public library's service to and ownership by the entire community, the generalist nature of the service it provides, and its neutrality make it a perfect environment for reconnecting specific groups and individuals with the community as a whole. If the strands of local community need to be rewoven, this process can take place at a variety of different connecting points. The public library should be one place of connection working with other connecting points to make a strong community. The public library should work to foster community identity, community dialogue, community collaboration, and community evaluation. Each of these functions will be described in the next chapter.

How This Developmental Model Differs from Private-Sector Models

The libertarian public library operates in a quasi-retail manner in which users are viewed as customers and services are developed in the same manner that the private sector develops market niches. Although library leaders can learn from private-sector development methodologies, it is extremely dangerous to ignore the important differences between public libraries and the private-sector institutions for which these methodologies were designed. The philosophy underlying these methods is contradictory to the public library's historic mission of education for a democratic society and antithetical to developing the library as a center of the community.

Customer Service Training and the Library As a Center of Community

Many public librarians have received training at customer service workshops in recent years. Those who attend these workshops rarely challenge the idea that the relationship of the public library with its users is essentially the same as the relationship between a business and its customers. The community movement's idea of balancing rights and responsibilities can help librarians see that the library's relationship with users is, in fact, very different from the relationship of a business with its customers.

Customers are empowered by conventional wisdom to be "always right" and hence without obligation to a business beyond the basic legal responsibility of paying for goods and services. Library users, however, have important responsibilities in the use and development of the public library. Library users, as citizens of the democracy, have a duty to become as fully educated and informed as possible. Unless citizens are willing to spend a great deal of personal money on books and other materials, this implies a responsibility to use the public library. Library users also have an obligation to use libraries in ways that will not hinder the use of this important service by other citizens. As taxpayers, library users have an obligation to adequately fund their public library through their taxes. The obligation to fund public libraries is especially clear for the officials who represent taxpayers in supporting public libraries. Public libraries should not treat users as customers, but as partners in the important work of strengthening the democracy.

This partnership with library users implies not only greater responsibilities for library users but also greater respect and consideration from the library staff than library users often receive. Although treating library users as customers is inappropriate, it does have the advantage of promoting friendlier treatment than is often provided by governmental institutions. An indifferent tolerance based on a citizen's right to use the library is certainly unsuitable for the relationship between librarians and library users.

At the Communitarian Summit in Washington, D. C., in 1999, Scott H. Moore presented an essay titled "Cultivating Hospitality: An Alternative to Tolerance in Political Discourse." Moore argued that tolerance is a weak virtue in that it is abstract and passive. Hospitality is a preferable ideal due to its concrete, active nature.[5] Hospitality can be measured because it requires various types of activity. This concept of active hospitality should be applied in the context of general service in public libraries. The bond between the library staff and the community should be stronger than the mere tolerance of people who have the legal right to use the library just as it should be stronger than the institutional self-interest that underlies the customer service ethic. Public libraries should be extending genuine hospitality rather than mere tolerance or customer service. Library users are not clients to be tolerated or customers to be exploited, but members of the community deserving love and respect. Library staff members are hosts and hostesses in a facility that in many ways functions as the community's living room.

Marketing and the Library As a Center of Community

Marketing is also based on a philosophy that is inappropriate to the public library. The techniques of marketing can be helpful in designing and publicizing our services; many public libraries have used these techniques to good effect. The basic idea of dividing the community into segments, however, can result in types of specialization inappropriate to the public library mission and destructive of the library's role as a center of community. The 1998 Public Library Association planning manuals, although positive in many respects, have been illustrative of the confusion that can occur when the marketing philosophy is indiscriminately applied to public library development.

In the introduction for *Planning for Results: A Public Library Transformation Process*, Sandra Nelson explains the influence of a Debra Wilcox Johnson study titled "An Evaluation of the Public Library Development Program" which was written in 1995. Nelson noted that, "The study provided critical information about the use of *Planning and Role Setting for Public Libraries* and *Output Measures for Public Libraries* . . . ." Nelson further explains that, "The Johnson study made it clear that although most public libraries (87 percent of those surveyed) had selected roles, fewer than 35% of those libraries had reallocated resources to support the roles they selected."[6] In the estimation of Ms. Nelson and the ReVision Committee, it was clear that the specialization of library services advocated by previous editions of the planning document had not gone far enough. This position represents the conventional wisdom, although apparently not the practice, of the profession.

Chapter 1 of *Planning for Results* offers the following advice: "Many libraries try to do too many things and end up doing many things inadequately instead of doing a few things well."[7] In the training session for *Planning for Results* at the Public Library Association's 1998 National Conference, Sandra Nelson explained that it would be appropriate to concentrate 80 percent of a public library's resources into three to five of the thirteen *service responses* suggested by the committee. These service responses included the following: basic literacy, business and career information, commons, community referral, consumer information, cultural awareness, current topics and titles, formal learning support, general information, government information, information literacy, lifelong learning, and local history and genealogy.[8]

The assumption in *Planning for Results*, as in the earlier PLA planning documents, is that the public library should not be a generalist

institution serving as wide a range of people as possible, but a specialized institution dominating a few market niches. The manual explains
that the mission of a library can be communicated by listing these market niches.

> The library's mission statement tells the community what business the li-
> brary is in. It says what the library does exceptionally well that is unique,
> or different, from what other agencies or organizations do. In *Planning
> for Results*, the library mission is a summary of the service responses
> your library has selected, written in words that are meaningful to the peo-
> ple of your community.[9]

Several important problems exist with this marketing-oriented approach to the mission of the public library. First, it assumes that there is
no basic mission of the public library as a national institution within
which local libraries should operate. Localities are free to reinvent the
institution without regard to the national institution. The service responses are presented with a relativistic indifference that devalues all of
the options. No advice concerning the intrinsic merit or weakness of
these options is offered. As in the private sector, it does not appear to
matter what is sold as long as the public likes it and will continue to
support the institution. Although common in the private sector, this is
inappropriate in the context of the public library. It should matter
greatly to librarians and trustees what type of service the public library
provides or elects not to provide. The future of both the local and national institution will depend upon the decisions that are made.

Second, a narrow specialization may mean that people in a variety of
market segments will not be served by the institution. If market segments are chosen, as they often are in the private sector, by their economic power and influence, those without service will tend to be the
poor and powerless. As with the selection of services, it makes a great
deal of difference how the public library defines its clientele. Fairness
in providing library service to the entire community is an important
principle that should be honored.

Third, to the extent that the public library is no longer of general
service to the community, it has lost the power to provide coordination
as a focal point for community consciousness and problem solving. The
assumption that strength comes from specialization is not true in the
case of the public library where power and authority are derived from
the library's status as a general community institution that serves everyone.

Fourth, the private-sector idea of developing and dominating market niches to obtain economic power supports competition rather than co-operation. Community organizations that offer services similar to those of the public library will tend to be viewed as competitors rather than as potential allies. In seeking to develop market niches, librarians seem to want to serve as the sole distributor for certain types of materials and services rather than as a community partner flexible enough to help in solving a variety of problems.

Conclusion

The public library is a center of the community and has a great potential to further serve communities by expanding this function. Communities are in desperate need for the civic space required for social interaction, dialogue, and collaboration. Communities need general, public places in a society dominated by specialization and privatization. The libertarian public library, however, reflects the weaknesses of the general culture rather than providing a life-giving response to these weaknesses. Library users are treated as customers who have the right to use the institution, but who have no responsibilities regarding the use or development of the library. Library services are provided in a quasi-retail fashion that encourages specialization and the domination of market niches. This pattern of development encourages competition and discourages collaboration with other community organizations.

Civic librarianship calls for library users to be treated as community partners who share the responsibility for the use and development of the library, not as clients to be tolerated or customers to be exploited. The library staff's relationship with users should be characterized by the active hospitality offered to friends and neighbors who share community membership.

Civic librarianship calls for public libraries to be active problem-solving agencies working in collaboration with other community organizations and individuals to improve community life. Library services need to be organized according to the changing individual and social needs of the community rather than according to the market niches that librarians believe can be most effectively exploited. It is not enough for public libraries to be passive materials distribution centers. Both the heritage of the public library and the present need for educational services require much more from one of America's most important institutions.

Notes

1. Redmond Kathleen Molz and Phyllis Dain, *Civic Space/Cyberspace: The American Public Library in the Information Age* (Cambridge, Mass.: MIT Press, 1999), 205-6.

2. William Fulton, "Rebuilding a Sense of Community," *Los Angeles Times*, 9 August 1998, 1(M).

3. Fulton, "Rebuilding a Sense of Community," 1(M).

4. Dean E. Murphy, "Moving Beyond 'Shh' (and Books) at Libraries," *New York Times*, 7 March 2001, East Coast late edition.

5. Scott H. Moore, "Hospitality As an Alternative to Tolerance" (paper presented at the 1999 Communitarian Summit of the Communitarian Network, Washington, D.C., February 1999), 5.

6. Ethel Himmel and William James Wilson, *Planning for Results: A Public Library Transformation Process; The Guidebook* (Chicago: American Library Association, 1998), vi.

7. Himmel and Wilson, *Planning for Results*, 3.

8. Himmel and Wilson, *Planning for Results*, 54.

9. Himmel and Wilson, *Planning for Results*, 31.

8

Strategies for Building Communities

How can public libraries help reweave the web of community? The systems development cycle, which underlies long-range planning, provides one way to organize public library strategies for community building. The systems development cycle in its most basic form includes studying the existing system, designing the new system, implementing the new system, and evaluating the new system. The cycle repeats in a natural transition as the evaluation of the new system leads to the beginning step of studying the existing system. The new system, of course, now is the existing system.

It may be helpful to translate this into the more familiar language of organizational long-range planning. Studying the existing system is a combination of studying the external environment and studying the internal workings of the organization. The mission statement is the fundamental expression of the organization's service to the external environment. Taken together, the goals and objectives developed in a long-range plan constitute the design of the new system. Implementation is the achievement of goals and objectives. Evaluation of the results of system changes is critically important because the means chosen to define success may either strengthen or weaken the real impact of service.

This development cycle works for organizations of all sizes. It is a good model for community development as well as for library development. As communities become engaged in formal long-range planning, public libraries should, of course, be involved. The types of community building strategies suggested here, however, are ways in which public libraries can contribute to the day-to-day development of community consciousness and problem solving that may or may not be a formal part of long-range planning at the community level. The community building services suggested here are ongoing services of the public library. These services can help to foster community identity, community dialogue, community collaboration, and community evaluation. In this chapter each of these strategies will be discussed in relation to the community's cycle of development.

It should be noted that these services are interrelated just as the steps of the systems development cycle are interrelated. For example, one way to foster a sense of community identity would be to present a program on local history that includes an element of public dialogue. Such a program could be developed in collaboration with other community groups and might contribute to the process of community evaluation if community problems and successes are discussed.

Community Identity

Studying the local community identity is analogous to studying the existing system in the systems development cycle. Communities cannot effectively improve themselves if community members do not understand the many facets of community identity. Individual community members are lost and disoriented without an understanding of community identity. Public libraries can help to foster community identity by offering materials, services, and programs related to the history, natural environment, economics, government, organizations and social structures, culture and the arts, and any other characteristics that define the community. The identity of the local community includes both local components and components from the larger environment of the community. State, regional, national, and international factors influence local identity as well as local factors.

As in studying the existing system in long-range planning, fostering a sense of community identity is especially important to community development. Knowledge of a community's identity is a necessary prerequisite to establishing a mission for the community. The mission is in effect a compact statement or understanding of identity that is developed through dialogue. Some level of consensus concerning community identity is a necessary foundation for community cooperation.

Whether this mission is formally articulated or not, it is necessary before developmental progress can be made. The public library is ideally positioned to offer services that promote the understanding of community identity. It is much easier to reach consensus concerning community identity when everyone has an accurate knowledge of the various facets of identity. This is a worthy educational project for public libraries.

Community Dialogue

Civic dialogue, as the community movement reminds us, is critically important in a democracy. In systems development terms, civic dialogue is the process by which a community designs its new system by setting new goals and objectives. This important democratic process is often given very little emphasis in public libraries despite the library's role as a limited public forum and despite the "Library Bill of Rights" proclamation that the library is an "institution for democratic living."[1] Librarians and trustees assume that their role in civic dialogue is limited to the provision of information. Although library leaders do not object to civic dialogue taking place in a library's meeting room, they do not believe that it is their job to encourage such discussions. The community movement suggests that it is everyone's job to promote civic dialogue. As the public library is committed to neutrality and as it belongs to and serves the entire community, the library is an ideal civic space for the promotion of public dialogue.

There are a wide variety of strategies that a public library could use to encourage civic dialogue. Public libraries can sponsor lectures and public meetings on community issues as well as candidate forums to prepare citizens for elections. Where other groups sponsor such events, the library can offer its meeting rooms as locations for these events. The library can present programs on such subjects to individual civic groups. Public libraries can also promote the general use of meeting rooms by a wide range of community groups. This use strengthens the community by encouraging dialogue as it strengthens the library's role as a center of the community. The interaction of individuals can be encouraged by providing space and encouragement for this to happen. This type of civic space can be provided online through electronic discussion groups devoted to civic issues, through rooms for group study, or in the form of a place for general social interaction such as a coffee bar or lounge. Strategies for promoting community dialogue will be further explored in the following chapter.

Community Collaboration

Community collaboration corresponds to implementing the new system in the systems development cycle. Public libraries should be far more alert to the possibilities for collaborations and partnerships to solve community problems. As a central community agency that is committed to neutrality, the public library is well positioned to facilitate such collaborative efforts. The community movement has encouraged finding solutions to public problems through extensive networks of collaboration. Successes in this type of collaboration, such as many of the community policing experiments, have provided proof of the effectiveness of this strategy.

Although this idea is not new to public librarians, the potential for seeing library services in the context of community collaboration is just beginning to show results. Public libraries vary tremendously in the frequency and effectiveness of collaborative efforts. Many public librarians do not see the usefulness of cooperating with agencies that are potential competitors. Utilitarian individualism encourages librarians and trustees to view their institutions as isolated institutions vying for a limited number of market niches. Many other public libraries have been influenced by federal and private foundation grant application instructions that encourage or require collaboration with other community agencies. In some cases, grant successes have encouraged an institutional philosophy of collaboration that has profoundly changed the management of the library.

A philosophy of collaboration that pervasively influences all aspects of library management is a key component of civic librarianship. This approach requires that public libraries participate in networks of civic agencies and organizations that monitor community needs and provide mutual support in meeting these needs. A central position in the community, a long history of neutrality, a powerful base of community information, and the availability of public meeting space makes the public library an ideal organization to encourage the formation of such a civic network if such an organization does not exist.

Such a structure for collaboration will allow powerful new strategies for solving community problems to emerge. This has been proven many times during successful experiments in collaboration during the

1990s. Examples of collaborative successes and advice concerning their duplication abound in the literature of the community movement and in the literature of the many professions, including librarianship, that have been influenced by this philosophy.

The great successes made possible through collaboration have shocked many people who have assumed that social problems such as high crime rates are intractable. In addition to exacerbating many types of social problems by encouraging antisocial behavior, the libertarianism of the 1980s argued against social efforts to correct these problems. This pessimistic point of view contributed profoundly to the sharp decline in public library outreach efforts after the aggressive efforts of the late 1960s and early 1970s. The practical success of the community movement's philosophy of collaboration has been a reminder that problems can be solved through collective effort. Americans are beginning to relearn the lessons of the generation that overcame the Great Depression and prevailed in World War II. Progress can be made in confronting even the most formidable problems if people work together to achieve the common good. The community movement reminds the nation that this is the American way, not individualism unbounded by social responsibility.

The most likely sources for public library collaboration are those organizations that are most closely aligned with the public library's mission of education for a democratic society. These institutions include schools, community and technical colleges, and four-year colleges and universities. Local government provides some types of public education as well as opportunities for participation in civic life. Local print and broadcast media have an important role in providing education and encouraging involvement in civic life. Beyond these obvious sources for collaboration are a myriad of public-sector, private-sector, and not-for-profit agencies and organizations that are available for assistance in addressing specific community needs. These community resources are underutilized by the vast majority of public libraries.

Especially interesting opportunities may arise where professionals in other areas of community service are interested in the ideas of the community movement. Newspaper publishers interested in civic journalism, police chiefs interested in community policing, and school superintendents interested in civic education and character development are increasingly common throughout the nation. Those interested in these trends within their own profession are especially likely to welcome a collaborative alliance with the public library. Becoming familiar with the ways in which other professions have used community movement ideas will allow library leaders to enter into a productive dialogue with potentially important allies.

Community Evaluation

Evaluation, the last step before the systems development cycle begins again, is also included in this list of community building services. How well is the community meeting its goals and objectives? It is important for community members to fully understand community successes as well as community problems. This understanding is related to community identity, but places a special emphasis on the effectiveness of community efforts toward improvement. Accurate, comprehensive information is needed to assist communities in undertaking this important dialogue. The most important sources of such information are the many planning documents, survey results, and statistical studies developed by community organizations of all types. Often community planning takes place in the fragmented context of specialized organizations that fail to study the community in a comprehensive way or fail to share their findings with the public. If it fails to fully involve the community in its planning efforts, local government itself may be functioning as such a specialized organization.

There is great potential for public libraries to assist in community evaluation by integrating and communicating the results of specialized community planning efforts. The public library could serve as a central resource for community-planning information. Collecting the planning information of private organizations, when it is available, could be especially useful as private-sector planning efforts are often better funded than those in government and not-for-profit agencies. In addition to aiding the process of community evaluation, collecting community-planning documents would help to avoid costly duplication of planning efforts and help to decrease the use of inaccurate information. Library leaders would benefit greatly from using this comprehensive planning resource in their own long-range planning.

Public libraries can also help communities utilize forms of evaluation that measure outcomes or results in addition to measuring organizational activity in the pursuit of results. The real impact of community service activities must be measured to provide accountability for public support. As Robin Volkmann notes in a recent article in the journal *Fund Raising Management,*

As organizations strive to maintain quality of service in an increasingly competitive environment, the ability to continuously improve is a necessity and outcome measurement is an effective tool to accomplish this.

Can a service organization answer the question, "Do we really make a difference in the lives of people?" Most can readily report on how much money they receive, how they disbursed it, how many clients they service and the number of hours spent serving them. However, more often than not, organizations cannot report on what eventually happens to the participants of their programs as a result of the services provided to them. . . .

As we move into the new century, a new trend is afoot for service organizations to focus on outcome measurements rather than historical numeric data. Those that support non-profit businesses are increasingly demanding to see not just proof that money is spent, but that it was spent effectively. For example, in a program that works to match troubled children with permanent adoptive families, the important question is no longer how many children were part of the program, but how many children were placed and stayed in their adoptive home.[2]

This new approach to measuring results is demanding, but necessary for service organizations of all types. It has great potential to assist public libraries. The use of outcome measures by not-for-profit organizations as well as the type of cost-benefit analysis performed in recent years by St. Louis Public Library point the way toward a new era of evaluation for public libraries and the communities they serve.

Conclusion

The public library can serve as a center of the community in a variety of important ways. Public libraries can help foster community identity by offering materials, services, and programs related to community characteristics such as history, economic, the arts, and the natural environment. Community dialogue can be fostered by public libraries that sponsor lectures and discussions on civic issues or simply provide meeting room space for community organizations and lounge areas for informal social interaction. The public library can encourage collaborative efforts to solve community problems by providing the information resources, meeting room space, and leadership to help organize such efforts. Public libraries can also help in the critically important area of evaluating the strengths and weaknesses of the community. Public libraries can assist the evaluation process by serving as a clearinghouse for local planning information and by assisting the community in new evaluation techniques such as outcome measurement.

Notes

1. American Library Association, "Library Bill of Rights," 1999, http://www.ala.org/work/freedom/lbr.html (29 October 1999).

2. Robin Volkmann, "Outcomes Measurement: The New Accounting Standard for Service Organizations," *Fund Raising Management* 30, no. 9 (November 1999): 26.

9

Library Services in a Social Context

To build communities through public library service, librarians and trustees must respond to the social dimension of community life. The libertarian perspective, which tends to view communities as collections of autonomous individuals, ignores the fact that human beings are social animals. The welfare of individuals cannot be separated from the welfare of the social systems that protect individual life. As community movement writers note, individual rights themselves exist only where they are supported by society. If the public library does not respond to social needs, it cannot be successful in responding to the needs of individuals. The institution must rest on both of the "pillars of the American way" noted in the 1947 *ALA National Plan*. The public library must address both "the democratic process of group life and the sanctity of the individual person."[1] Success in developing library services and success in obtaining library support both depend on balancing attention to individuals with attention to groups.

This chapter will begin with a general discussion of the need to meet social needs. The political advantages that service to groups can offer for building support for the public library will next be discussed. This section will be followed by a discussion of how serving groups can improve public library service. Developing public libraries will be shown to be a political process.

The Libertarian Bias against Serving Groups

Although the public library has a long tradition of serving groups in a community context, the current libertarian ideology tends to view the institution as an isolated organization that serves individuals. The ideology of the libertarian public library views other service organizations as potential competitors rather than as collaborators. The libertarian public library's focus on meeting the public's demand for information places a great stress on the circulation of materials to individuals. To restore the social dimension of public library service, public librarians and trustees need to view the institution as a member of a community service network that educates both individuals and groups in a variety of ways.

Due to limited resources, it is, of course, necessary for public librarians and trustees to establish rigorous service priorities. The Public Library Association's planning process manuals are right in advising that public libraries cannot be all things to all people. The planning process manuals are wrong, however, in two important ways. First, they demonstrate a bias against services that are either provided by community coalitions or directed toward groups of people. This arbitrarily reduces the potential services to be offered and removes from consideration some services that might be granted high-priority status. Although moderated somewhat in *Planning for Results*, this bias remains an important part of the planning process tradition.

Second, the planning process manuals suggest that priorities should be established according to the service market niches, described as roles or service responses, that the planning committee wishes to pursue rather than according to the specific problems a community needs to solve. Community needs are considered to be needs for general types of service rather than needs to solve particular problems. Although *Planning for Results* begins to move toward a more social model of public library service, this movement is powerfully contradicted by its increased dedication to cultivating specialized market niches as a developmental strategy.

The radical individualism of the libertarian public library places unnecessary limitations on the types of services that the public library might provide. Public librarians and trustees should consider a full range of institutional responses to community needs rather than arbitrarily limiting the public library to those services to individuals that can be achieved without the help of other organizations. When public librarians and trustees arbitrarily decide that a social problem affecting groups of people is too large for the library to address, they preclude the possibility of a collaborative project in which the public library could make an important contribution. When library leaders decide to serve only individual users, they rule out services to groups of people that may be more useful to individuals than the current services the library provides. The primary purpose of serving groups is to enhance the library's service impact for both groups and individuals.

One example of the current bias against service to groups is the low priority given to public programming in most public libraries. Service to groups is often viewed as a public relations effort to strengthen the real focus of the library, service to individuals. Although some libraries offer musical concerts for their communities, for example, most would prefer to loan music recordings to individuals. The potential popularity of live music in libraries and the inherent superiority of delivering the service in this manner are often not considered in establishing service priorities. Public librarians and trustees simply do not believe that providing services of this type is their responsibility.

In addition to collaborating with other agencies on social service projects and providing educational programs in a social setting, the public library can provide a place for formal and informal social interaction. As suggested earlier, formal social interaction can be encouraged by library sponsored programs that encourage dialogue and interaction. Formal interaction can also be promoted by encouraging the use of library meeting rooms by community organizations and by otherwise assisting these organizations. Civic librarianship as envisioned here would consider such services to be much more important than they are in the libertarian public library.

Community movement writers such as Robert Bellah remind Americans that the contribution of associations and groups of all kinds vitally enriches democratic life. Bellah and his associates explain in *Habits of the Heart* that Alexis De Tocqueville noted the importance of these groups to American democracy in his early visits to this country.

> In ways that Jefferson would have understood, Tocqueville argues that a variety of active civic organizations are the key to American democracy . . . . Associations, along with decentralized, local administration, mediate between the individual and the centralized state, providing forums in which opinion can be publicly and intelligently shaped and the subtle habits of public initiative and responsibility learned and passed on.[2]

In addition to promoting the formal interaction of organized groups, the public library should promote the type of informal social interaction that receives too little support in most American communities. Ray Oldenburg writes about the need for a "third realm of satisfaction and social cohesion beyond the portals of home and work" that offers "essential element of the good life" in many other societies. He analyzes the powerful, but subtle contributions of places of informal social interaction in his book *The Great Good Place.* Oldenburg notes that suburban America is especially lacking in "a generous proliferation of core settings of informal public life."[3]

As with the formal provision of civic space in a community, the public library cannot provide all of the informal public space needed for a healthy community. The public library can make an important contribution to solving this problem, however. Current trends in library buildings indicate an increased use of group study areas and coffee bar lounge areas. An important contribution of *Planning for Results* is the recognition that serving as a "commons" is a possible service response for public libraries.[4] A library facility designed from the perspective of civic librarianship might make the commons area of the lounge a focal point for the institution and increase the size of such an area to make this a more substantial service.

The community movement encourages library leaders to find ways to support the social environment that go well beyond the cursory efforts of most public libraries. In addition to the general community-building strategies of the previous chapter and the basic perspective just described, a more detailed strategy is required to help library leaders study and support the social life of our communities. The best way to approach this complex problem is through the specific community groups and organizations present in the local community. Working with groups is essentially a political process, but one based upon effective service. The usefulness of serving groups to gaining community support will be discussed first because this benefit often dominates the discussion of service to groups. The more basic and important service advantages of working with groups will follow this discussion.

Service to Groups and Political Power

In analyzing the groups in a community, public librarians and trustees should begin by studying the nature of the public library itself. The interaction of the public library with community groups constitutes just as much of a political process as it does for any other governmental organization. This basic fact of life is often overlooked to the detriment of the institution. As Oliver Garceau notes at the conclusion of his book *The Public Library and the Political Process*, public librarians are hurt by their inability to come to grips with the inherently political nature of the public library's governmental context.

> Much of the literature of the profession and many of the research interviews have operated on the inarticulate premise that public libraries are private business, somehow in mortal danger of contamination by contact with government. To the student of the political relations of the public library this is a most important fact about public library attitudes. By and large, public librarians are not thinking of themselves as employees of government or department heads in a public bureaucracy. They are nevertheless inescapably involved in "politics." It is the conclusion of our research that it is of paramount importance to librarians, to library service, and to the citizen that public librarians understand and appreciate more clearly the political world of the public library.[5]

This problem, which Garceau noted in 1949, intensified with the ascendance of the utilitarian individualism of the libertarian public library in the 1980s. The philosophy of private sector development strategies is not only inappropriate to public library development; it is a dangerous distraction from the political work required to sustain the institution.

Garceau supported the efforts of those public libraries that attempted "to mobilize community support by library participation in group activities." Garceau cites Denver Public Library as a successful example of the political impact of providing service to groups. In describing Denver Public Library in 1949, Garceau notes that the library director organized an educational consortium that, in addition to the public library, included "the library of the municipal university, a library school, a regional bibliographic center, and the Adult Education Council." The director and the library staff were also actively involved in a wide range of community organizations of all types. Garceau writes, "His staff has followed his lead and affiliated with a much longer and more improbable list of clubs, committees, councils, centers, associations, commissions, leagues, campaigns, conferences, and fraternities." The library provided staffing to maintain systematic contact with over two thousand community groups to make sure that their library service needs were met.[6]

Garceau does not present the Denver Public Library example as typical of public libraries of the time. Although public library interaction with groups was by no means rare, it was unusual to find such an outstanding example. Garceau criticized most public libraries for their lack of involvement with groups and believed that this lack of involvement contributed to weak funding. Although he acknowledges that his survey cannot prove a correlation between service to groups and public support, he writes, "But it must be said in passing, and only for its suggestive worth, that the one library of the survey that is admittedly embarrassed by its riches from public taxation has as extensive a program of group services as the ingenuity of man can dream of."[7]

Edward Howard, former director of Vigo County Public Library in Indiana, also criticized the inactivity of most public libraries in serving groups. His 1978 book *Local Power and the Community Library* provides a conceptual framework for analyzing the power structure of a community by taking an inventory of "government, independent, private, and voluntary" organizations.[8] Howard provides a detailed methodology for organizing library support through service to influential groups. As in the case of Garceau, Howard's focus is on developing public support rather than on providing community service.

Power, Service, and the
Danger of Goal Displacement

The perspective of Garceau and Howard is important and true. Serving groups is a powerful technique for strengthening community support. As a strategy for gaining support, this approach is more appropriate to the governmental nature of the public library than the private-sector methodologies discussed in the previous chapter. Garceau and Howard place library development in the context of community organizing and politics rather than in the context of developing market niches.

It is important to note, however, that even appropriate strategies for gaining support must be subordinate to the first priority of the public library, service to the community. This distinction and its consequences for the institution are all too often not recognized by public librarians and trustees. In his book *Modern Organizations* Amitai Etzioni explains the phenomenon of *goal displacement*. He writes that goal displacement occurs most commonly when organization leaders become "concerned more with preserving and building up the organization itself than in helping it to serve its initial purpose."[9]

Public librarians and trustees need to understand that the long-term success of the public library must be based on a solid foundation of effective service and that their efforts to build public support must not compromise the services that their libraries provide. If they approach service to groups strictly as a means to gain public support, it is clear, for example, that the library will stress service to those groups with power rather than service to less powerful groups that may be in greater need of the services they provide. This is the type of thinking that led to the Public Library Inquiry's recommendation to serve only an elite group of active, well-educated citizens. Such an approach results in goal displacement. The public library was created to expand public involvement in education and participation in civic life, not simply to tend to the needs of educated citizens already active in civic life.

How Serving Groups Can
Improve Public Library Service

The real potential of serving groups is the improvement of public library service, the foundation for any increase in public support for the institution. Service to groups can improve public library service by offering powerful conduits for information to flow between the library and community members. This new communication can aid libraries by providing a more detailed understanding of community needs, by offering a context for ongoing library user education tailored to specific interests, by providing access to community expertise for the development of collections and services, and by opening up new possibilities for collaboration and resource sharing. These powerful benefits to library service provide a foundation for the political advantages suggested by Garceau and Howard, but are worth pursuing whether or not public support in the form of library funding is the result.

The types of advantages to be gained from service to groups can be illustrated by the relationship that many public libraries have with local genealogical societies. The close ties that such groups often have with public libraries result in some or all of the benefits mentioned above. These groups tell librarians what they need and often assist in the funding and development of the appropriate collections or services. The active presence of the genealogical society members in the library increases the likelihood that the library will provide specialized user education to this group. Society members may also help the library by providing user education and individual assistance in genealogical service to the general public. If library funding is threatened, members of the genealogical society are prime candidates for support because they understand the importance of a strong library to their interests. The relationship between Ohio public libraries and genealogy societies is described in some detail in Donald Litzer's article "Library and Genealogical Society Cooperation in Developing Local Genealogical Services and Collections."[10]

Although this type of beneficial relationship could exist between the public library and other groups, the inactivity of public libraries in interacting with groups has precluded this from happening. The genealogical society-public library relationship itself would not have developed in most communities without the request for this relationship from the genealogical society.

Conclusion

To effectively serve their communities, library leaders must offer services and collections that meet both social needs and the needs of individuals. The welfare of individuals cannot be separated from the social systems that support individual life. The ideology of the libertarian public library ignores the social dimension of community life to the detriment of both society and the individual. This ideology carries with it a bias toward service to individuals provided by the library as an individual organization. Civic librarianship as envisioned here is supportive of both services to groups and collaborations with other organizations when such services and collaborations can best meet the library service needs of the community. Services to groups and collaborations with other organizations can benefit the public library by increasing political support. The primary benefits of providing services in a group context, however, are the many possibilities for mutual support that relationships with groups can offer. The library is strong politically and as a service provider to the extent that the institution cultivates positive relationships with those it serves. Many of these people can best be reached through community groups.

Notes

1. Oliver Garceau et al., *The Public Library in the Political Process* (Boston: Gregg Press, 1972), 144.

2. Robert N. Bellah et al., *Habits of the Heart: Individualism and Commitment in American Life* (Berkeley: University of California Press, 1996), 38.

3. Ray Oldenburg, *The Great Good Place: Cafes, Coffee Shops, Community Centers, Beauty Parlors, General Stores, Bars, Hangouts and How They Get You through the Day* (New York: Paragon House, 1989), 9, 15.

4. Ethel Himmel and William James Wilson, *Planning for Results: A Public Library Transformation Process; The Guidebook* (Chicago: American Library Association, 1998), 54.

5. Garceau, *Public Library*, 238-39.

6. Garceau, *Public Library*, 138, 138, 138, 139.

7. Garceau, *Public Library*, 140.

8. Edward N. Howard, "Local Power and the Community Library," *Public Library Reporter* 18, (1978): 5.

9. Amitai Etzioni, *Modern Organizations* (Englewood Cliffs, N.J.: Prentice-Hall, 1964), 10.

10. Donald S. Litzer, "Library and Genealogical Society Cooperation in Developing Local Genealogical Services and Collections," *Reference & User Services Quarterly* 37, no. 1 (Fall 1997): 37-52.

10

Strengthening Library Politics

As the development of library services and support is essentially a political process, it is extremely important that library leaders approach this effort with a clear political platform. The restoration of the social authority of library leaders and the renewal of the public library mission of education for a democratic society are fundamental to developing such a political platform. Library leaders must be clear about both the importance of the purpose of the institution and their right as social authorities to pursue this purpose. To effectively function in today's highly competitive political atmosphere, library leaders must also develop stronger political positions and more powerfully promote these positions. This chapter will demonstrate the inadequacies of the politics of the libertarian public library and offer a new approach to library politics that supports the institution's commitment to the seemingly contradictory principles of advocacy and neutrality.

The Politics of the Libertarian Public Library

The libertarian public library, like the libertarian social consensus of the 1980s, combines the expressive individualism of the Left and the utilitarian individualism of the Right. This combination of motivations has resulted in a strange mixture of passion and indifference. The expressive individualism of the New Left lives on in the intense promotion of divisive social positions that are often held by only a small percentage of American citizens. This is a politics that uses the relativism of modernism against social purposes to promote individual liberty. This approach to politics is disinterested in the moral concerns of society, but highly moralistic whenever social concerns threaten to curb individual freedom. This adversary culture stance is, in some instances, limited to activist members of American Library Association's Social Responsibilities Round Table. At other times, the promotion of such positions receives a much broader base of support among library leaders.

Library leaders, as representatives of a neutral public agency, should not take sides in the culture wars. They have done so, however, at the national level. In keeping with expressive individualism, the culture war allies of the library leadership are the most strident exponents of the adversary culture that began with Romanticism and continued through the various forms of modernism. These allies include the motion picture industry, the American Civil Liberties Union, the arts establishment, Playboy Enterprises, Internet libertarians, and many writers and academics. Culture war enemies of the library leadership include the Christian Coalition, the *Wall Street Journal*, Laura Schlessinger, and the millions of citizens who do not share the values of the adversary culture.

The more typical reaction of public librarians and trustees at the local level is one characterized by the neutrality of indifference. Utilitarian individualism sells a service; it is not interested in social morality. This indifference to the welfare of society precludes public criticism of the Boy Scouts' position on gay rights as well as a passionate defense of the usefulness of public libraries as a means of education for the democracy. Neither the divisive politics of expressive individualism, which often violates institutional neutrality nor the moral indifference of utilitarian individualism, which fails to support any type of advocacy, will succeed. A strong, but unifying library politics that supports both advocacy and neutrality is required. Public libraries need to actively address the great issues of the culture wars in even-handed and unifying ways, not as strident combatants or disinterested relativists. This section will demonstrate the inadequacies of library politics based on expressive and utilitarian individualism.

Expressive Individualism and Advocacy for Children's Rights

No example of public library advocacy has been more damaging to the institution than the defense of the rights of children to use the public library in opposition to parental rights, the concerns of the general society, and common sense. This professional position has become controversial in the 1990s due to problems with the use of the Internet. The public library's position on children rights has been flawed, however, since "age" was included in the "Library Bill of Rights" as one of the reasons why a person's right to use a library should not be "denied or abridged."[1] The extreme promotion of children's rights has been one of expressive individualism's most divisive and dysfunctional positions.

Seeing children as autonomous individuals rather than incomplete creatures requiring special rules and support is a quintessentially Romantic belief. To return to an important quote from E. D. Hirsch Jr., "Romanticism concluded that the child is neither a scaled-down, ignorant version of the adult nor a formless piece of clay in need of molding, rather, the child is a special being in its own right with unique, trustworthy—indeed holy—impulses that should be allowed to develop and run their course." Hirsch explains that, "The idea that civilization has a corrupting rather than a benign, uplifting, virtue-enhancing effect on the young child is a distinct contribution of European Romanticism to American thought."[2] If children are, as Wordsworth and other Romantics believed, in many ways superior to adults, it follows that the efforts to civilize them are likely to be damaging and counterproductive. This idea, as explained in earlier chapters, strikes at the legitimacy of society's efforts to educate the young and undermines the role of the public library as an educational institution serving society. The Romantic understanding of childhood is as lacking in viability as anarchism is lacking as a form of government.

The impracticality of the "Library Bill of Rights" prohibition against denying or abridging library service due to age has been obvious from its inception. Many library administrators have found themselves unwilling to allow unsupervised children to use library meeting rooms. They have also been unwilling to allow expensive equipment of various types to be borrowed by children. Almost everyone understands that children are not ready for some types of responsibility. Librarians have insisted, however, as Herbert White noted in a 1999 letter to *American Libraries* on Internet filtering that, "children are only vertically challenged adults, with exactly the same rights."[3]

This belief in children receiving the same rights as adults is extremely unlikely to prevail in the court of public opinion or in the judicial system as Internet filtering challenges are heard. Similarly, if a child's right to keep library records confidential from her or his parents is challenged in the courts, the statutes supporting this "right" are likely to be overturned. Amitai Etzioni's 1998 *Wall Street Journal* editorial addressed the civil libertarian position on children's rights.

> The ACLU's determination to give minors the rights adults enjoy is a perversion of freedom. Underlying a free society is the assumption that individuals have a basic ability to render judgments. But we aren't born with that ability; children gradually develop it. For this reason, we are not charged with violating children's right to free assembly when we prevent them from running into the street, or their privacy rights when we examine their homework.[4]

The extreme position taken by many librarians on the rights of children is an example of a mistake in framing the philosophical position of the institution that can create unnecessary problems. This mistake illustrates the important truth that being aggressive advocates is not enough; library leaders must advocate workable positions that correspond with reality. If the basic framework of the democracy and the basic framework of the public library are, in fact, threatened, library leaders must, of course, support the framework regardless of public popularity. Before they risk the future of the institution, however, library leaders should make sure that their view of the world is appropriate. In the case of the extreme promotion of children's rights, a wide variety of groups and individuals have been deeply disturbed by this untenable political position. As Herbert White explained in the aforementioned letter, "This will continue to cost us dearly in goodwill, unless you simply want to dismiss the *Wall Street Journal* as a right-wing rag. We need *WSJ*'s support, but we go to extremes to alienate anyone who might favor a middle ground."[5]

Utilitarian Individualism and the Neutrality of Indifference

Although neutrality is an important value for the public library, the indifference of relativism is an inappropriate moral basis for an institution dedicated to improving the community. An important distinction needs to be made between the type of neutrality that is based upon relativistic indifference and a neutrality that is based upon respect for everyone's point of view in a pluralistic society. Relativism, as noted earlier, treats ideas as personal preferences and, in doing so, devalues personal and social decision making. Education can make sense only where it is understood that some ideas are, in fact, better than others and that decisions can have important consequences for good or ill.

Warren A. Nord and Charles C. Haynes explain this important distinction in their book *Taking Religion Seriously across the Curriculum*.

> Many times, in dealing with controversial topics, we've heard teachers say, "There is no right answer." Sometimes, in their concern to be tolerant, teachers will say that all religions are fundamentally the same beneath their outward differences. Much of the multicultural movement emphasizes the (equal) respect due all traditions. And, as we have argued, for educational and constitutional reasons public schools, texts, and teachers must remain neutral on matters of religion.
>
> Not surprisingly, many religious folk interpret all of this as relativism—the idea that no religion (or point of view generally) is any better or truer than any other. One of the most difficult tasks teachers have is to convey to students the difference between pluralism (and a tolerance or respect for people holding different views) on the one hand, and relativism on the other.
>
> It is important to remember—and to remind students—that the disagreements among different religious and secular traditions are about *what the truth is*. If students come to believe that choosing a religious (or political or scientific) position is like choosing what to eat from a buffet line, they will have misunderstood the nature of religion (and science) badly. From within each tradition, some foods are poisonous; others are healthy; and individuals certainly should not choose them on the basis of appearances or taste.[6]

Nord and Haynes note that, "Neutrality cannot mean hostility or even silence." Neutrality, they believe, requires that we "must take everyone seriously" as a demonstration of fairness and respect.[7] Warren Nord expands on these ideas in his book *Religion & American Education: Rethinking a National Dilemma*.

> Historically, political liberalism has underwritten a constitutional framework that allows people to live together peacefully in spite of their deep differences. Properly understood, it should provide a point of agreement between secular and religious folk who disagree about what is ultimately important and how to make sense of the world. Because our culture is so deeply divided, public education should not take sides in our culture wars but should maintain neutrality, treating the contending alternatives fairly. Indeed, *only by taking each other seriously* can we resolve our national dilemma about religion and education.[8]

The preceding discussion of relativism and pluralism applies to public libraries as well as public schools. Public institutions should not exacerbate the real differences among Americans by either taking sides or silently ignoring the need to resolve these differences. Haynes and Nord are right when they call for an active, positive neutrality that respects both the variety of viewpoints and the people who express these points of view. There is important listening to be done by all sides in the great culture war debate. The public library cannot be a neutral place for this listening to occur if it is identified with one side of the argument.

The Politics of the Libertarian Public Library As a Failure in Both Advocacy and Neutrality

The politics of the libertarian public library fails to be effective as an expression of either advocacy or neutrality. The advocacy of expressive individualism failed for the New Left as it failed for the Democratic Party during the 1970s and 1980s. This failure was due to inherent weaknesses in the positions taken as well as to the adversary culture's habit of seeking out unpopular positions with the express purpose of angering mainstream society. This self-defeating approach to political action has resulted in many library leaders either quietly or openly operating their institutions in ways that oppose the views of large segments of the communities that they serve. The politics of expressive individualism, as practiced by library leaders, cannot succeed as advocacy because it is weak in presenting the philosophical framework of the institution and because it violates the institution's neutrality. Weakness in presenting the philosophical framework of the institution is due primarily to the fact that expressive individualism does not believe in the mission of education for a democratic society. Weakness in neutrality is the result of believing that society must always be fought as the enemy of individual liberty.

The politics of the libertarian public library that is based upon utilitarian individualism also fails to support the institution. The amoral relativism of this position avoids political advocacy altogether and replaces it with the bottom line of the marketplace, the distribution of products and services. Utilitarian individualism does encourage neutrality on issues of social morality. This neutrality, however, is based on a passive disinterest in the welfare of society that is inappropriate for an institution of public education.

Civic Librarianship and Library Politics

How can the public library maintain a strong position of advocacy while preserving the neutrality of the institution? Must library leaders choose between taking sides on every social issue or avoiding all expressions of the social good? The public library has a simultaneous need for political advocacy to promote the work of the institution and for political neutrality as an institution that serves everyone in the community. This paradox is basic to the social context of the public library. The ideas of the community movement can help library leaders find an appropriate balance between advocacy and neutrality.

Amitai Etzioni describes America's pluralistic society as a mosaic in which the different pieces are held together by a frame and glue.[9] The laws and traditions of American democracy provide the philosophical framework that allows the multiplicity of specific groups and individuals to work together as one society. By extension, the public library is supported by a framework of laws and traditions that allows all members of society to be served. It may be helpful, if somewhat oversimplified, to look at the philosophical framework of the public library as the place for advocacy, the place for communicating the social values of the institution, and the selection of materials and services as the place for neutrality, the place for fairness and respect to specific groups and individuals. The value of neutrality is, of course, itself an important part of the philosophical framework. It is also true that the selection of materials and services constitutes a type of advocacy.

The community movement understands that a good society is characterized by a high level of both rights and responsibilities. In keeping with this idea, public librarians and trustees need to be much stronger in promoting both the rights of specific groups and individuals to receive service based on friendly neutrality and the responsibilities that everyone shares within the institutional framework of the public library. It is as inappropriate to take a position on every social issue that presents itself as it is to be silent in defending the basic framework of the institution as a social good. Both the neutrality and the advocacy of library leaders need to be more consistent and more active.

It is clear that the libertarian public library offers library leaders two dysfunctional political options, the failed politics of the New Left, which has already been abandoned by the Democratic Party, or the relativistic indifference to the welfare of society that is characteristic of the marketplace. A return to the public library's historic mission of providing education for a democratic society can help library leaders to clarify the philosophical and political framework of the organization. If this is done, both library leaders and the general public will be better able to understand how the public library can balance advocacy and neutrality to promote stronger, more unified communities. A new, more activist library politics based upon the mission of education for a democratic society is necessary to counter the antigovernment, antisocial challenges to the public library presented by libertarian politics at all levels of government. These challenges provide a legitimate opportunity for advocacy as they represent a very real attack on the importance of public education as a support for democracy.

Countering the Libertarian Argument

The loss of the mission of education for a democratic society presents a serious problem for the political promotion of the public library. This problem exists with local funding bodies as well as with legislative bodies at the state and national levels. The libertarian political position in its pure form is not interested in providing public funding for social projects beyond the bare bones of military support, police support, and the basic infrastructure necessary for economic life. Many libertarians consider funding for public education to be the responsibility of those using this service, not the general public. Libertarians often suggest that public libraries should be funded entirely by a combination of user fees and philanthropy. As libertarian ideas are now common in the Republican Party, many public librarians and trustees are familiar with this line of reasoning. Despite the fact that tax support for public libraries is the result of the failure of user fees and philanthropy to finance the institution, support for this approach has gained popularity not only among the general public but also among librarians and trustees.

Part of the dysfunction of the current political efforts of public librarians and trustees is due to the inability of library leaders to counter the libertarian argument. The inadequacy of defending the institution against libertarian opposition with the tools of the libertarian public library is evident whenever librarians and trustees are challenged as being morally wrong to ask those who do not use the library to help pay for it. Library leaders might respond that library "A" loans 500,000 items, answers 75,000 information requests, and presents programs attended by 15,000 people each year. Furthermore library "A" received a 98 percent approval rating for general satisfaction in a recent citizen survey. The obvious counter to the arguments of high use and popularity is that no important public purpose is being served by this high use and popularity. Politicians can explain that, although a restaurant with free food would be heavily used and extremely popular, it does not follow that such an institution should receive tax support. No longer armed with the commanding public purpose of education for a democratic society, the libertarian public library is defenseless against such a criticism. The moral challenge of libertarianism must be met with a moral defense, not talk of activity and popularity.

Ultimately the solution to the political problem posed by libertarianism is the difficult process of educating and leading by exercising the social authority of the institution. If a large portion of the public considers the public library to be the answer to a question it no longer asks, it is the job of library leaders to explain that the success of the democracy still depends on making good decisions, making good decisions still depends on public education, and public education still depends, in part, on the public library. The public library can succeed in its mission of education for a democratic society only where people believe in working together to improve society through democratic institutions. Where this understanding and commitment has been lost, it is the job of library leaders to work with others to rebuild this understanding and commitment. The public library is a community institution. Where commitment to the community is lost, the public library will be lost.

In his book *Is There a Public for Public Schools?*, David Mathews makes a parallel argument regarding the public schools in noting the "erosion of the historic commitment to the idea of schools for the benefit of the entire community."[10]

> Why doesn't "engaging the public" go far enough? That is, there may be so few people supportive of the idea of public schools—so small a community for these inherently community institutions—that school reform may need to be recast as community building. In other words, certain things may have to happen in our communities before we can see the improvements we want in our schools.[11]

Community building is necessary to provide an atmosphere supportive of public education just as public education is a vital component of community building.

Perhaps the best way to counter the libertarian challenge to social purposes in general and public education in particular is to join with other groups in developing services that prove the value of public libraries to communities. Although political coalition building in recent years has often reflected the politics of expressive individualism, there are indications that a wiser approach to building alliances is underway which attempts to establish coalitions based upon a mutual interest in public education. Sarah Ann Long developed many positive new educational partnerships for the American Library Association during 1999-2000. The Urban Library Council's work with the Benton Foundation has been a positive collaboration in support of public education. The non-profit organization Libraries for the Future has encouraged collaboration with foundations. Still much more could be done to strengthen the public library through political collaboration. All through the 1990s public libraries missed opportunities for foundation grants and governmental funding available for those willing to embrace the developmental strategies of the community movement. Powerful coalitions with law enforcement, journalism, and the other professions in which community movement ideas have gained influence are still waiting to be forged.

Conclusion

Library leaders need to be confident and strong in their advocacy for the mission of the public library. This confidence and strength has been diminished in the libertarian public library by reduced support for public education and the right of social authorities to pursue this purpose. The incoherent politics of the libertarian public library vacillates between the often-misdirected passion of New Left-style expressive individualism and the social indifference of the marketplace that is characteristic of utilitarian individualism. Advocacy that does not honor the neutrality of the library as a public institution is as inappropriate as an indifferent neutrality that is unable to speak for the institution.

Civic librarianship offers a new balance between advocacy and neutrality that is based on a clearer view of the responsibilities everyone shares for supporting the public library as well as the rights of specific groups and individuals to receive fair treatment as library users. Advocacy needs to be based on the purposeful and publicly supported mission of education for a democratic society. Neutrality needs to be respectful of different points of view and the people who hold these points of view as well as actively involved in providing a forum in which differences may be discussed. Library politics, as Jean Lipman-Blumen recommends for all organizations, needs "to move beyond a politics of differences to a politics of commonalities."[12] Such a political perspective is necessary if public libraries are to successfully meet libertarian challenges to library funding and build coalitions with other groups committed to public education.

Notes

1. American Library Association, "Library Bill of Rights," 1999, http://www.ala.org/work/freedom/lbr.html (29 October 1999).

2. E. D. Hirsch Jr., *The Schools We Need; And Why We Don't Have Them* (New York: Doubleday, 1996), 74, 75.

3. Herbert S. White, "Seeking Middle Ground," *American Libraries* 30, no.11 (December 1999): 32.

4. Amitai Etzioni, "ACLU Favors Porn Over Parents," *Wall Street Journal*, 14 October 1998, 22(A).

5. White, "Seeking Middle Ground," 32.

6. Warren A. Nord and Charles C. Haynes, *Taking Religion Seriously across the Curriculum* (Alexandria, Va.: Association for Supervision and Curriculum Development, 1998), 53-54.

7. Nord and Haynes, *Taking Religion Seriously*, 18, 19.

8. Warren A. Nord, *Religion & American Education: Rethinking a National Dilemma* (Chapel Hill: University of North Carolina Press, 1995), 8.

9. Amitai Etzioni, *The New Golden Rule: Community and Morality in a Democratic Society* (New York: Basic Books, 1996), 192.

10. David Mathews, *Is There a Public for Public Schools?* (Dayton, Ohio: Kettering Foundation Press, 1996), 2.

11. Mathews, *Is There a Public*, 3.

12. Jean Lipman-Blumen, *Connective Leadership: Managing in a Changing World* (Oxford: Oxford University Press, 1996), 335.

11

Specific Professional Concerns

Civic librarianship offers a philosophical framework and a plan of action that are very different from those of the libertarian public library. The previous chapters have given a general description of these differences with illustrative references to professional concerns and public library services. In this chapter, the potential implications of civic librarianship to specific professional concerns and library services will be offered in additional detail. Although more detail is necessary to demonstrate the power of this paradigm, it should be noted that the meaning of this new perspective for public librarianship is under construction.

Civic librarianship is based on both an older tradition of public library service that is no longer understood and a new approach to the public library as a community resource that is not yet fully understood. Those interested in civic librarianship are exploring both a lost world and a new continent. The goal here is not so much to provide a detailed description of civic librarianship, but to encourage those who might wish to explore this new approach to public library development. If these ideas are to deeply benefit public librarianship, they will need to be tested and developed throughout the nation. This is precisely what has happened in professions such as journalism and law enforcement in which the perspective of the community movement has had a powerful influence.

Professional concerns to be discussed in this chapter will include education for public librarianship, the recruitment and retention of public librarians and trustees, developing collections and services, popular materials, and library facilities and outreach services.

Education for Public Librarianship

One of the great benefits of civic librarianship is that it places the emphasis on the impact that library services have on individuals and society. The work of librarianship, which is often viewed as abstract and theoretical, is judged in the realm of real life outcomes for the individuals and communities that libraries serve. Civic librarianship encourages public librarians and trustees to understand the importance of public education to the democracy and to take community problems very seriously.

Unfortunately this respect for the application of ideas in the interest of public service is declining in support. The most telling example of this trend is the debate among library science educators concerning the use of the term "library" in the names of schools of library and information science. The reluctance to use the term "library" reflects, in part, an interest in gaining status within the university where theory is valued over practice and academic research is valued over professional training.

Don Fallis and Martin Fricke present a rationale for the decline of practical education for librarianship at the graduate level in their 1999 article "Not by Library School Alone." They affirm: "Practical skills training is not graduate-level education." They further conclude that, "Widespread introduction of practical skills courses at the graduate level would conflict with the mission of the university, the school, and, ultimately, library science itself."[1]

Two problems exist with this otherwise plausible argument. First, professional education in public administration, education, medicine, and law addresses practical issues as well as theory. Second, the assumption that a librarian can successfully fulfill the practical duties of a professional with an assortment of undergraduate skills is demeaning to the reality of the work. Fallis and Fricke are no doubt correct that some types of practical work should not be taught in graduate school. If the public library is an important part of public education and if public education is critically important to the democracy, it would seem, however, that education in this vital practice should be enriched rather than degraded. Any public library director who is sensitive to the many complex demands of long-range planning, for example, knows that the practice of librarianship is often much more demanding and complex than the practical education librarians receive in graduate school.

Eliminating the reference to libraries in the names of professional schools is far from a simple matter of semantics. It is a major step in a long process of valuing theory over practice and arid expertise over public service. This is an understandable, if lamentable, response to the culture of the contemporary university. In a 1999 article, Bill Crowley and Bill Brace note that this response is a rejection of the historical service rationale for land grant public universities.

> Transformations of schools of library and information science into schools of information have mostly occurred against the wishes of the many members of the affected library, media, and information communities. Such change is difficult to challenge in private institutions, but the situation is different in public institutions. The reason is the pervasive influence of a particularly American institution: university commitment to responsiveness, service, and outreach.[2]

Crowley and Brace explain that the movement away from public service to abstract information is also due to the rhetoric of practicing librarians and the American Library Association that reduces the profession's focus to information rather than supporting a broader educational mission.

> Several decades of linking the fate of libraries, library media centers, and information centers to the concept of information are now exacting a price.
> If information is the only game in town, the wonder is not that schools of information are proliferating; rather, the marvel is that any ALA-accredited program retains the word "library" in its name. Pick your cliché: "Sow the wind, reap the whirlwind," or "Live by, die by." When you assert that information is the heart and soul of your library, media, or information center operations, don't be surprised when former library and information science faculty see the future as information-only education for students. If the profession keeps telling educators to "listen to the customer" and "follow the market," don't be surprised if we do.[3]

The social purpose of education for a democratic society is denied by both the public library and the university resulting in the abandonment of the historical commitments that form the rationale for these institutions.

Civic librarianship encourages the renewal of the historical commitment to education and public service. Because it holds this demanding and extremely complex purpose, civic librarianship justifies a complex preparation worthy of graduate-level courses. The libertarian mission of providing access to information for individuals is a much less demanding pursuit that fails to justify graduate education. The real problem underlying professional education for librarians is that the profession is abandoning the mission that provided the initial rationale for graduate education for librarians.

The Recruitment and Retention of Public Librarians and Trustees

It is often difficult to recruit and retain highly qualified people to serve as public librarians and trustees. For paid positions, the highly competitive current job market is a contributing factor. Deeper problems exist, however, due to the change in the mission of the public library. A noneducational public library no longer has an inspiring mission that requires the best efforts of highly educated people. Degrading the mission degrades the work both in terms of the motivation to do the work and in terms of the substance of the work itself. This is complicated by denying the social authority necessary to perform the traditional function.

Kay S. Hymowitz writes of the devalued role of the teacher and its impact on retention of classroom teachers.

It may also be that the coach-teacher is an irresistible ideal in a society which places autonomy on the top of its list of virtues and which is increasingly ambivalent about childhood. But whatever the cause, one can begin to see why the profession has been plagued by a 50 percent attrition rate in the first five years of work. Why would adults want to be teachers in a society that believes adults have nothing to teach?[4]

The parallel question for librarians and trustees is obvious. "Why would anyone want to dedicate their efforts to an educational institution that does not seek to educate?" This is an especially powerful question for potential candidates for librarianship. If the public library is not actively trying to strengthen communities through education, why should a highly qualified person be interested in this work? As salaries are low relative to many other professions, libraries rely on the idealism of this work to recruit and retain professional librarians. In the case of trustees, idealism is literally the only attraction as no financial compensation is offered. The basis for idealism is eroded as the educational mission is displaced. The restoration of the social authority of library leaders and the institution's educational mission would powerfully contribute to the recruitment and retention of librarians and trustees.

Developing Collections and Services

According to the ideology of the libertarian public library, the public library exists for the purpose of presenting a broad range of personal expression. This view is clearly stated in a recent memorandum from the Jenner and Block law firm to the American Library Association that cites "the primary library mission of providing access to a broad and diverse range of materials."[5] This view of the institution is strikingly different from the traditional view that education is the primary purpose of the public library. In the traditional view, providing a broad range of expression is a means of education, not a mission for the institution. The one-sided view of the public library as a provider of access is typical of the libertarian public library in that it acknowledges individual freedom while ignoring the social purposes of education.

A more balanced view of freedom of expression in the context of the public library is provided by Robert Leigh in *The Public Library in the United States*. Leigh describes freedom of speech in the context of the public library in the following manner.

> The constitutional right of a free press in the United States is specifically the right to publish their ideas unhindered by governmental limitation. . . . At the same time, the assumption behind government activities is that they shall promote public order, morality, and decency. The public library, therefore, cannot escape the responsibility either for careful selection on the basis of quality or for maintaining the widest possible area of free communication. It must reject, but may not censor.[6]

It is the charge of the public library to provide a broad range of individual expression within an educational framework that is supportive of the community.

The high seriousness of the Public Library Inquiry led these researchers to stress *quality* rather than *demand* in the traditional debate over materials selection. As noted earlier, the ideology of the libertarian public library has advocated that demand be the primary criterion for selection and is very distrustful of librarians exercising their social authority to select quality materials. Civic librarianship suggests a balance between quality and demand that is similar to the balance between the community framework for library service and the range of individual expression.

The pursuit of quality in selection should not be viewed, however, in terms of absolute standards of academic or cultural quality. Civic librarianship is oriented toward positive educational results for individuals and solving problems for communities. Such results will require materials representing a range of complexity to meet the needs of the wide variety of developmental leveles found in any community. At each level of complexity, librarians are called upon to use their expertise to choose the materials that will be most useful. Such choices are decisions in favor of quality and are intended to educate. This essential professional activity is, of course, one important reason why society requires a high level of education to perform materials selection.

The general development of collections and other services is a process of attending to the needs of individuals, groups, and the community as a whole. The range of expression must be maintained through a commitment to neutrality; the positive social presence of the public library must be maintained through support for the public good. It is the responsibility of public librarians and trustees to provide library service in the best way possible by balancing these often-contradictory charges. Library leaders are required to construct a social framework for the range of individual expression that comports with the constitutional requirements. Whether the framework chosen for selection is detailed in a collection development plan or exists only in the minds of selectors, the public library cannot avoid this responsibility.

Popular Materials

One of the most explosive controversies in public library history has been the debate over the presence of light fiction. Patrick Williams describes this controversy as it existed between the years 1876-1896 in his book *The Public Library and the Problem of Purpose.*

> During those same years, the professional community came to realize that the public's preference for books of little or no educational value was an enduring one. Librarians ceased to believe in the taste-elevation theory, which argued that books of little or not educational value should be supplied to library users because such books are necessary at the earliest stage of self-education. They are attractive to readers who otherwise

would read nothing. If such books are supplied, their readers will gradually lose their taste for them and demand books of educational value.

During the last quarter of the nineteenth century, as disbelief in the taste-elevation theory spread, librarians engaged in a long controversy over what to do about popular fiction.[7]

Williams quotes several influential librarians of the time who powerfully opposed the demand-oriented materials selection that encouraged the purchase of popular fiction. He notes that William I. Fletcher, a public librarian from Connecticut, wrote that, "The managers of the public library are no less bound to control and shape the institution in their charge . . . than are the managers of the school system. To say that calls for books should be accepted as the indications of what should be furnished, is to make their office a merely mechanical and perfunctory one."[8] Williams supplies a similar quote from William F. Poole.

> Our public libraries and our public schools are supported by the same constituencies, by the same methods of taxation, and for the same purpose; and that purpose is the education of the people. For no other object would a general tax for the support of public libraries be justifiable. If public libraries shall, in my day, cease to be educational institutions, and serve only to amuse the people and help them to while away an idle hour, I shall favor their abolition.[9]

In 1950 Robert Leigh, Oliver Garceau, and the other authors of the Public Library agreed with Fletcher and Poole in viewing the public library as an educational institution with a responsibility to control the quality of materials selection. As Douglas Raber noted in his book *Librarianship and Legitimacy: The Ideology of the Public Library Inquiry*: "That the public library might someday base its legitimacy precisely on its ability to satisfy public demand is a condition that could scarcely be imagined by the authors and supporters of the Inquiry."[10]

These powerful defenses of the educational function of the public library made by Fletcher, Poole, and the authors of the Public Library Inquiry are well taken and congruous with the serious educational mission for the public library that is recommended here. The mission of the public library is serious, educational, and vital to the welfare of both individuals and the community. The conclusion, however, that such an institution should not provide popular fiction is unwarranted. If the premise is accepted that quality decisions can be made at all levels of complexity, it is possible to defend the idea of supplying the simpler forms of fiction.

Part of the problem stems from the traditional idea that fiction is not artistic or cultural, but merely a form of entertainment or recreation. This traditional idea should be questioned in all areas of popular materials. For decades early in his career, Duke Ellington's jazz music was appreciated in America as dance music while he was honored as a great composer in Europe. This and countless other examples should convince us that popular culture is not always inferior to high culture. Many novelists have clearly achieved a high level of art. These artistic achievements were often initially considered mere entertainment.

Popular fiction and other materials also have a community building function that should be taken very seriously. The creative arts are powerful representations of cultural identity. A society's cultural identity is reflected and shaped by the narratives found in fiction and other popular art forms. At the local, regional, and national levels, the stories people tell are more powerful than the tools they use. This is so because the cultural narrative directs a society's mission and this mission directs the use of tools. Artistic narratives, however simple in nature, are vital to the development of individuals and the larger communities to which they belong. If library leaders look at fiction and other popular materials in this light, they will realize that these materials have an important place in the public library. This place is one that must be balanced, however, with the other legitimate educational tasks of the institution. A simple surrender to the demand approach to selection will clearly degrade the mission of the public library.

Library Facilities and Outreach Services

An important goal of civic librarianship is to create civic space for community development. Civic librarianship values the public library as a place for social interaction and community building as well as a place for the education of individuals. If library leaders honor the social dimension of public library service, they will value current library facilities differently and plan new facilities that reflect this priority. Some of the possible implications include increasing the number and size of public meeting rooms and auditoriums, adding rooms for group study, and developing coffee bars and other types of commons areas. Even relatively small library branches might benefit from having space for social interaction to allow them to function as centers of local communities and neighborhoods.

Community movement ideas are extremely supportive of library outreach efforts designed to solve important community problems. Civic librarianship views solving the problems of the community as an important reason for supplying educational resources. Collaboration with other service agencies and groups is a powerful approach to seemingly intractable community problems. The many successful collaborations in law enforcement and social work which have been developed using community movement ideas should give public librarians and trustees new optimism and interest in outreach services. The public library can contribute to the solution to problems such as crime and homelessness, but is not strong enough to approach such problems without extensive support from others. Success in solving such problems benefits the library as well as the community as a whole.

The many problems resulting from homelessness, for example, have been extremely damaging to the atmosphere of urban libraries. Anything that can be done to alleviate this problem will greatly benefit public libraries suffering from this problem. It is time for public librarians and trustees to exercise their underutilized outreach muscles. It is a time for renewed optimism, hope, and the hard work of building communities.

Notes

1. Don Fallis and Martin Fricke, "Not by Library School Alone," *Library Journal* 124, no. 17 (15 October 1999): 45.

2. Bill Crowley and Bill Brace, "A Choice of Futures: Is It Libraries versus Information?" *American Libraries* 30, no.4 (April 1999): 79.

3. Crowley and Brace, "Choice of Futures," 76.

4. Kay S. Hymowitz, *Ready or Not: Why Treating Children As Small Adults Endangers Their Future—and Ours* (New York: Free Press, 1999), 84.

5. Jenner and Block, "Internet Filtering in Public Libraries," Memorandum to American Library Association 2000, http://www.ftrf.org/internetfiltering memo.html (4 February 2000).

6. Robert D. Leigh, *The Public Library in the United States* (New York: Columbia University Press, 1950), 116-17.

7. Patrick Williams, *The American Public Library and the Problem of Purpose* (New York: Greenwood Press, 1988), 9.

8. Williams, *American Public Library*, 11.

9. Williams, *American Public Library*, 10.

10. Douglas Raber, *Librarianship and Legitimacy: The Ideology of the Public Library Inquiry* (Westport, Conn.: Greenwood Press, 1997), 13.

12

The Future of the Public Library

Civic librarianship seeks to strengthen communities through developmental strategies that renew the public library's mission of education for a democratic society. Civic librarianship reaffirms the traditional mission of the public library and offers powerful new strategies for community development through library service. In judging the appropriateness of civic librarianship to the future development of the public library, the following two questions must be answered. What will American society be like in the future? Will the reforms of civic librarianship effectively serve the needs of this future society?

This chapter begins with an assessment of the movement toward reintegration in American society and the general advantages that library leaders may gain through conforming to this cultural shift. The reforms of the civic librarianship will next be discussed relative to their potential future success. The chapter will conclude with final words concerning civic librarianship and the future development of public libraries and their communities.

The Great Reintegration
and Civic Librarianship

Is America destined for a long decline into increasing individualism, cultural fragmentation, and confusion in which the culture becomes progressively less concerned about the shared values of social morality? Will America become stronger and more coherent as a society as it finds a new balance between individual autonomy and social order? What will the future hold?

American society is undergoing a fundamental change in direction. After thirty years of disorientation and extreme challenges to social purposes, social authorities, and norms of behavior, the nation has begun to find its balance again. A new balance between society and the individual is beginning to bring the reassertion of social purposes, the restoration of social authority, and new respect for norms of behavior. Decades of social disintegration will now be followed by a period of reintegration. Francis Fukuyama marks the beginning of this change as dating from the early to mid-1990s when sociological indicators of disintegration such as crime rates began to decline.[1] E. J. Dionne Jr. marks the beginning of a political shift from libertarian politics toward a new progressivism as dating from 1995.[2] If Jesse Shera is right that "the objectives of the public library are directly dependent upon the objectives of society,"[3] a very large change is in store for the public library. This change may be as significant as the transformation resulting from the cultural civil war.

Will American society return to the cultural atmosphere existing before 1965? Will the American public library return to its pre-1965 form? It is obvious that whatever transformation occurs in the coming years cannot be a simple return to a bygone era. This transformation will, however, include elements of the past that were too quickly discarded during the rapid cultural change of recent decades. Society would benefit, for example, from a renewed respect for the role of public education in a democratic society and a renewed respect for the role of the public library as an institution of public education. Will respect and support for the public library increase in the years ahead? The answer to this question depends not only on social trends but also on the leadership of public librarians and trustees.

If American society is moving in the direction of social reintegration, there are too basic types of advantages for library leaders in adapting to this cultural change. First, it is always easier to move in the direction of a social current. Second, the direction of this current is entirely positive for public library development. This cultural shift strengthens social purposes, empowers social authorities, and stresses the importance of public education. The adaptation to the ideology of the libertarian public library in recent decades has had the advantage of allowing library leaders to move in the direction of the prevailing social current. That advantage is being lost, however, as the culture begins to move in the opposite direction. The ideology of the libertarian public library has not had the second advantage of providing support for the institution. The libertarian ideology's combination of hostility and indifference toward social purposes in general and public education in particular makes this ideology a weak basis for public library development.

Library leaders already find themselves in conflict with a society that is focusing on reestablishing norms of social conduct rather than further expanding individual rights. This problem is demonstrated by the American Library Association's conflict with radio host Dr. Laura Schlessinger over Internet filtering. Francis Fukuyama places the popularity of Schlessinger in a cultural context.

> Any number of other signs suggest that culturally, the period of ever-expanding individualism is coming to an end, and that at least some of the norms swept away during the Great Disruption are being restored. In the 1990s, one of the biggest phenomena in daytime radio in the United States is a call-in show hosted by Dr. Laura Schlessinger. . . . Her message could not be more different from that of the generation of liberationist therapists who in the 1960s and 1970s advised people to "get in touch with their feelings" and discard social constraints that would stand in the way of "personal growth."[4]

Library leaders have mistakenly believed that Laura Schlessinger is merely an eccentric and ephemeral public figure. From the perspective of the libertarian politics of the 1980s, Schlessinger might be viewed as a troublesome, but marginal religious conservative at the fringe of American culture. If Fukuyama is right about Schlessinger's importance, however, library leaders are in conflict with the increasingly dominant flow of the culture. Such a conflict is, of course, a much more serious matter. Not seeing the cultural paradigm shift that is underway is already weakening the ability of library leaders to respond effectively to such challenges.

Conforming to the cultural shift now underway can do much more than help library leaders avoid trouble. The emerging dominance of the community movement perspective offers new opportunities for support.

The dedication of library leaders to the libertarian paradigm during the 1990s has greatly restricted effective alliances with agencies of the federal government that have been influenced by community movement ideas, has minimized the support for libraries from the many foundations receptive to communitarian innovation, and has left undeveloped potentially fruitful collaborations with journalism, law enforcement, and the public schools that might have been developed around communitarian themes.

The communitarian perspective of civic librarianship has the advantage of being in tune with the dominant flow of the culture and in tune with the essential mission that the public library has pursued throughout its history. There is no need to deny the governmental, social, educational, and generalist nature of the institution. Library leaders can be in the much more comfortable position of affirming rather than denying the tradition of public librarianship.

The Reforms of Civic Librarianship and the Future of the Public Library

Restoring the Social Authority of Public Librarians and Trustees

Under the ideology of the libertarian public library, library leaders have been forced to try to lead without leading and educate without educating. Civic librarianship frees library leaders to once again exercise their social authority as educators, administrators, and leaders. The weakening of the social authority of public librarians and trustees in recent decades has damaged the institution's ability to provide services and to compete for funding in an increasingly competitive social environment. The voices of library leaders have been softened both by society's declining support for social authorities and public education and by personal doubts concerning the appropriateness of serving as educators, administrators, and leaders. Community movement ideas can help reestablish the confidence public librarians and trustees need to fulfill these demanding responsibilities with power and effectiveness. No one can be optimistic about the future of the public library if the confidence of public librarians and trustees in exercising social authority is not restored.

Renewing the Mission of Providing Education for a Democratic Society

Education for a democratic society is now and always has been the mission of the public library. This is so despite the movement of the libertarian public library to a mission of access to information for individuals. Recent surveys of public opinion indicate that both average citizens and community leaders view the public library as an educational institution. While the public continues to expect public libraries to be social institutions that acquire high-quality educational materials and services, public librarians and trustees have been developing quasi-retail operations directed by popular demand and unconcerned with social purposes.

Technological advances, as everyone would agree, will provide rapidly increasing access to information in the future. Public libraries should make educational use of these advances to the extent this can be done with limited public funding. As Robert Leigh noted in the Public Library Inquiry, however, competing with large private corporations as a noneducational distributor of materials is futile considering the strength of the public library relative to these corporations.[5] Education has been left largely to the public sector because it is an extremely complex and time-consuming process with a low profit margin. Education is an attractive mission for the public library because it is highly beneficial, indeed vital to communities. Education is more useful than ever in a society where access to information is increasingly available and the educational support necessary to sorting through these resources is lacking. Public libraries that provide only access to information will be increasingly unnecessary in the future.

Developing the Public Library As a Center of the Community

The community movement identifies an increasingly important need for places for civic dialogue and informal social interaction. Public libraries have been serving these purposes, but could find a greatly expanded role for such services in a society that is interested in coming together after decades of increasing isolation. Private-sector developmental models will be more and more dysfunctional in a more communitarian society. Developing public libraries as if they are retail stores, however, has never been the road to institutional strength as it makes the institution redundant and unnecessary. A more communitarian society will require that library users be treated as partners in using and developing the institution rather than as customers separate from the library. Library resources will need to be marshaled to solve community problems rather than organized to secure dominance in specialized market niches. The public library will need to collaborate with community organizations to solve problems rather than compete for market share. As David Mathews writes in reference to the public schools, public libraries will need to be "embedded in a rich civic network" if they are to thrive in the future.[6]

Developing Strategies to Build Communities

A future in which communities are coming together is one in which public libraries will be valued for the many ways they can support the process of community building. Community movement strategies such as fostering community identity, community dialogue, community collaboration, and community evaluation offer powerful and interrelated methods to strengthen both the community and the library. Providing support for these functions by offering materials, services, public programs, meeting rooms, staff expertise, and leadership are important ways in which public libraries can help to strengthen communities.

Providing Library Services in a Social Context

It is likely that the trends toward increased competition for public funds and increased accountability in the use of these funds will continue. If this is so, it will be very important for public libraries to understand the full range of a community's library service needs as well as the full range of community resources available for responding to these needs. To make the best use of public library resources, services to groups must be considered as well as services to individuals.

Serving groups is a powerful means of improving both library services and political support through increased community contact and communication. Serving groups may improve library services by providing a more detailed understanding of community needs, by offering a context for library user education tailored to specific interests, by providing access to community expertise for developing library collections, and by providing new opportunities for collaboration and resource sharing. Serving groups is an appropriate response to the fact that the public library is a governmental institution that is developed through political means, rather than a private business developed through marketing techniques. As individuals depend on groups and the communities as a whole for support, it is impossible to provide optimal service to individuals without regard for the social context of individual life. Collaborations with other community groups will be an increasingly important feature of institutional life for public libraries.

Strengthening Library Politics

The politics of the libertarian public library vacillates between hostility and indifference to social needs depending on the relative influence of expressive and utilitarian individualism. The aggressively antisocial politics of expressive individualism is divisive and often encourages the violation of the public library's tradition of neutrality. Expressive individualism is also inadequate in its advocacy of basic institutional values, in part because it does not believe in these values. The indifference to social needs of utilitarian individualism reflects the amorality of the marketplace and is entirely inappropriate for a social institution.

Library leaders must be confident and strong in their advocacy for the public library. The first steps toward this confidence and strength are the restoration of the social authority of library leaders and the renewal of the public library mission of education for a democratic society. A clear purpose will help public librarians and trustees to find a new balance of advocacy and neutrality. The basic institutional values of the public library need to be more strongly advocated; library leaders also need to observe a more respectful neutrality on issues that are not of essential importance to the institution.

Library leaders need to understand that the library politics of the future will need to be unifying and pragmatic rather than divisive and theatrical. Avoiding politics altogether is also not an option for the public library. What is needed is an approach to library politics that unifies communities around the shared values of the democracy and actively seeks to provide a neutral forum for the resolution of community disagreements. Community movement ideas can help library leaders to counter libertarian attacks on public library funding as well as assist library leaders in building new coalitions to support public education.

Conclusion

Public librarianship has been hollowed out. Challenges to the social authority of library leaders and to the historic mission of the public library have weakened the institution in important ways over the past thirty years. After decades of extreme individualism, however, America is moving to strengthen its damaged social structures. Public libraries can be an important part of this life-giving process if library leaders seize this opportunity to renew the public library mission of education for a democratic society and find new ways to strengthen communities through library service. The ideas presented here as civic librarianship can be powerful tools in this process of institutional and community renewal.

The mission of the public library is the greatest purpose in a democracy, the mission of public education. It is time for library leaders to once again embrace this mission and to make full use of the many strengths of this great institution. There is exciting work to be done that can improve communities of all sizes. A new century has begun and the best days for America and America's public libraries are ahead.

Notes

1. Francis Fukuyama, *The Great Disruption: Human Nature and the Reconstitution of Social Order* (New York: Free Press, 1999), 271.

2. E. J. Dionne Jr., *Why Americans Hate Politics* (New York: Simon & Schuster, 1991), 228-29.

3. Jesse H. Shera, *Foundations of the Public Library: Origins of the Public Library Movement in New England 1629-1855* (Chicago: University of Chicago Press, 1949; n.p.: Shoe String Press, 1965), 248.

4. Fukuyama, *Great Disruption*, 272.

5. Robert D. Leigh, *The Public Library in the United States* (New York: Columbia University Press, 1950), 224.

6. David Mathews, *Is There a Public for Public Schools?* (Dayton, Ohio: Kettering Foundation Press, 1996), 19.

Bibliography

This is a selective list of resources. The topics discussed here relating to either the community movement or the public library are each represented by an extensive body of literature. The following titles provided major influences of one type or another on the development of this proposal for civic librarianship.

Barber, Benjamin. *A Place for Us: How to Make Society Civil and Democracy Strong.* New York: Hill & Wang, 1998.
Barker, Joel Arthur. *Paradigms: The Business of Discovering the Future.* New York: HarperCollins, 1992.
Bayles, Martha. *Hole in Our Soul: The Loss of Beauty and Meaning in American Popular Music.* Chicago: University of Chicago Press, 1994.
Bellah, Robert N., et al. *The Good Society.* New York: Vintage Books, 1992.
———. *Habits of the Heart: Individualism and Commitment in American Life.* Berkeley: University of California Press, 1996.
Berlin, Isaiah. *The Roots of Romanticism.* Princeton: Princeton University Press, 1999.
Berry, Wendell. *What Are People For?: Essays.* San Francisco: North Point Press, 1990.
Bloom, Allan. *The Closing of the American Mind.* New York: Simon & Schuster, 1987.
Boaz, David. *Libertarianism: A Primer.* New York: Free Press, 1997.

Broder, David S., and Richard Morlin. "Struggle over New Standards: Impeachment Reveals Nation's Changing Standards." *Washington Post*, 27 December 1998, 1(A).

Carter, Stephen L. *Civility: Manners, Morals, and the Etiquette of Democracy.* New York: Basic Books, 1998.

————. *The Culture of Disbelief: How American Law and Politics Trivialize Religious Devotion.* New York: Basic Books, 1993.

————. *Integrity.* New York: Basic Books, 1996.

"Children's Access: Protection or Preparation?" *American Libraries* 30, no. 10 (November 1999): 59-62.

Crowley, Bill, and Bill Brace. "A Choice of Futures: Is It Libraries versus Information?" *American Libraries* 30, no.4 (April 1999): 76-79.

D'Elia, George, and Eleanor Jo Rodger. "Public Opinion about the Roles of the Public Library in the Community: The Results of a Recent Gallup Poll." *Public Libraries* (January/February 1994), 23-28.

Dewey, John. *Democracy and Education: An Introduction to the Philosophy of Education.* New York: Free Press, 1944.

Dionne, E. J. Jr. *They Only Look Dead: Why Progressives Will Dominate the Next Political Era.* New York: Simon & Schuster, 1996.

————. *Why Americans Hate Politics.* New York: Simon & Schuster, 1991.

Ditzion, Sidney. *Arsenals of a Democratic Culture: A Social History of the American Public Library Movement in New England and the Middle States from 1850 to 1900.* Chicago: American Library Association, 1947.

Ehrenhalt, Alan. *The Lost City: Discovering the Forgotten Virtues of Community in the Chicago of the 1950s.* New York: Basic Books, 1995.

Etzioni, Amitai. "ACLU Favors Porn Over Parents." *Wall Street Journal*, 14 October 1998, 22(A).

————. *Modern Organizations.* Englewood Cliffs, N.J.: Prentice-Hall, 1964.

————. *New Communitarian Thinking: Persons, Virtues, Institutions, and Communities.* Charlottesville: University Press of Virginia, 1995.

————. *The New Golden Rule: Community and Morality in a Democratic Society.* New York: Basic Books, 1996.

————. *The Spirit of Community: The Reinvention of American Society.* New York: Simon & Schuster, 1993.

Fallis, Don, and Martin Fricke. "Not by Library School Alone." Library Journal 124, no. 17 (15 October 1999): 44-45.

Fukuyama, Francis. *The Great Disruption: Human Nature and the Reconstitution of Social Order.* New York: Free Press, 1999.

Fulton, William. "Rebuilding a Sense of Community." *Los Angeles Times*, 9 August 1998, 1(M).

Garceau, Oliver, et al. *The Public Library in the Political Process.* Boston: Gregg Press, 1972.

Garrison, Dee. *Apostles of Culture: The Public Librarian and American Society, 1876-1920.* New York: Free Press, 1979.

Glendon, Mary Ann. *Rights Talk: The Impoverishment of Political Discourse.* New York: Free Press, 1991.

Harris, Michael. "The Purpose of the American Public Library," *Library Journal* 98, no. 16 (15 September 1973): 2509-2514.

Himmel, Ethel, and William James Wilson. *Planning for Results: A Public Library Transformation Process; The Guidebook*. Chicago: American Library Association, 1998.

Hirsch, E. D., Jr. *The Schools We Need; And Why We Don't Have Them*. New York: Doubleday, 1996.

Holt, John. *Escape from Childhood*. New York: E. P. Dutton, 1974.

Howard, Edward N. "Local Power and the Community Library." *Public Library Reporter* 18 (1978): 1-56.

Hunter, James Davison. *Culture Wars: The Struggle to Define America*. New York: Basic Books, 1991.

Hymowitz, Kay S. *Ready or Not: Why Treating Children As Small Adults Endangers Their Future—and Ours*. New York: Free Press, 1999.

Isserman, Maurice, and Michael Kazin. *America Divided: The Civil War of the 1960s*. New York: Oxford University Press, 2000.

Jenner and Block, "Internet Filtering in Public Libraries," Memorandum to American Library Association 2000, http://www.ftrf.org/internetfiltering memo.html (4 February 2000).

Johnson, Alvin. *The Public Library: A People's University*. New York: American Association for Adult Education, 1938.

Jung, C. G. "Commentary." In *The Secret of the Golden Flower: A Chinese Book of Life*. New York: Harcourt, Brace & World, 1962.

Kunstler, James Howard. *Home from Nowhere: Remaking Our Everyday World for the Twenty-First Century*. New York: Simon & Schuster, 1996.

Lasch, Christopher. *The Culture of Narcissism: American Life in an Age of Diminishing Expectations*. New York: Norton, 1979.

————. *The Revolt of the Elites and the Betrayal of Democracy*. New York: Norton, 1995.

Leigh, Robert D. *The Public Library in the United States*. New York: Columbia University Press, 1950.

Lipman-Blumen, Jean. *Connective Leadership: Managing in a Changing World*. Oxford: Oxford University Press, 1996.

Litzer, Donald S. "Library and Genealogical Society Cooperation in Developing Local Genealogical Services and Collections." *Reference & User Services Quarterly* 37, no. 1 (Fall 1997): 37-52.

Louv, Richard. *Childhood's Future*. Boston: Houghton Mifflin, 1990.

————. *The Web of Life: Weaving the Values That Sustain Us*. Emeryville, Calif.: Conari Press, 1996.

Mathews, David. *Is There a Public for Public Schools?* Dayton, Ohio: Kettering Foundation Press, 1996.

McCook, Kathleen de la Peña. *A Place at the Table: Participating in Community Building*. Chicago and London: American Library Association, 2000.

Medved, Michael. *Hollywood vs. America: Popular Culture and the War on Traditional Values*. New York: HarperCollins, 1992.

Minow, Norman N., and Craig L. LaMay. *Abandoned in the Wasteland: Children, Television, and the First Amendment.* New York: Hill & Wang, 1995.

Molz, Redmond Kathleen, and Phyllis Dain. *Civic Space/Cyberspace: The American Public Library in the Information Age.* Cambridge, Mass.: MIT Press, 1999.

Moore, Scott H. "Hospitality as an Alternative to Tolerance." Paper presented at the 1999 Communitarian Summit of the Communitarian Network, Washington, D.C., February 1999.

Neill, A. S. *Summerhill: A Radical Approach to Child Rearing.* New York: Hart Publishing, 1960.

Nifong, Christina. "Cooperation Cuts a Community's Crime." *Christian Science Monitor* 89, no. 12 (11 December 1996): 1.

Nord, Warren A. *Religion & American Education: Rethinking a National Dilemma.* Chapel Hill: University of North Carolina Press, 1995.

Nord, Warren A., and Charles C. Haynes. *Taking Religion Seriously across the Curriculum.* Alexandria, Va.: Association for Supervision and Curriculum Development, 1998.

Oldenburg, Ray. *The Great Good Place: Cafes, Coffee Shops, Community Centers, Beauty Parlors, General Stores, Bars, Hangouts and How They Get You through the Day.* New York: Paragon House, 1989.

Padover, Saul K., ed. *The Complete Madison: His Basic Writings.* New York: Harper, 1953.

Palmour, Vernon E., Marcia C. Bellassai, and Nancy V. De Wath. *A Planning Process for Public Libraries.* Chicago: American Library Association, 1980.

Pattison, Robert. *The Triumph of Vulgarity: Rock Music in the Mirror of Romanticism.* New York: Oxford, 1987.

Peck, M. Scott. *A World Waiting to Be Born: Civility Rediscovered.* New York: Bantam Books, 1993.

Postman, Neil. *The End of Education: Redefining the Value of School.* New York: Vintage Books, 1995.

Public Library Association. *The Public Library Mission Statement and Its Imperatives for Service.* Chicago: American Library Association, 1979.

Purdy, Jedediah. *For Common Things: Irony, Trust, and Commitment in America Today.* New York: Alfred A. Knopf, 1999.

Putnam, Robert D. *Bowling Alone: The Collapse and Revival of American Community.* New York: Simon & Schuster, 2000.

Raber, Douglas. *Librarianship and Legitimacy: The Ideology of the Public Library Inquiry.* Westport, Conn.: Greenwood Press, 1997.

Rosen, Jay. "The Action of the Idea." In *The Idea of Public Journalism*, ed. Theodore L. Glasser. New York: Guilford Press, 1999.

Roszak, Theodore. *The Making of a Counter Culture: Reflections on the Technocratic Society and Its Youthful Opposition.* Garden City, N.Y.: Doubleday, 1969.

Schlesinger, Arthur M. Jr., *The Disuniting of America.* New York: Norton, 1992.

Schorr, Lisbeth B. *Common Purpose: Strengthening Families and Neighborhoods to Rebuild America.* New York: Anchor Books, 1997.

Schuman, Patricia Glass. "Speaking Up and Speaking Out: Ensuring Equity through Advocacy." *American Libraries* 30, no. 9 (October 1999): 50-53.

Shenk, David. *Data Smog: Surviving the Information Glut.* New York: HarperEdge, 1997.

Shera, Jesse H. "On the Value of Library History." In *Reader in American Library History,* ed. Michael H. Harris. Washington, D.C.: NCR Microcard Editions, 1971.

————. *Foundations of the Public Library: Origins of the Public Library Movement in New England 1629-1855.* Chicago: University of Chicago Press, 1949; n.p.: Shoe String Press, 1965.

Tannen, Deborah. *The Argument Culture: Stopping America's War of Words.* New York: Ballantine Books, 1998.

Tocqueville, Alexis de. *Democracy in America.* Ed. J. P. Mayer. Trans. George Lawrence. New York: HarperPerennial, 1988.

Volkmann, Robin. "Outcomes Measurement: The New Accounting Standard for Service Organizations." *Fund Raising Management* 30, no. 9 (November 1999).

White, Herbert S. "Seeking Middle Ground." *American Libraries* 30, no.11 (December 1999): 32.

Williams, Patrick. *The American Public Library and the Problem of Purpose.* New York: Greenwood Press, 1988.

Wilson, James Q. *The Moral Sense.* New York: Free Press, 1993.

Wolfe, Alan. *One Nation After All: What Middle-Class Americans Really Think about God, Country, Family, Racism, Welfare, Immigration, Homosexuality, Work, the Right, the Left, and Each Other.* New York: Viking Press, 1998.

Index

About the Author

Ronald B. McCabe (B.A., Luther College; M.S.L.S., University of Kentucky) has served five communities as a library leader and manager since joining the profession in 1975. He has worked as a branch librarian in Reidsville, North Carolina; and as a library director in Le Mars, Iowa; Moline, Illinois; Champaign, Illinois; and Wisconsin Rapids, Wisconsin. As director of McMillan Memorial Library in Wisconsin Rapids, he chaired the South Wood County United Way campaign in 1995, served as a member of the Board of Directors of the Wisconsin Rapids Rotary Club, and has been active in a variety of other community organizations. In 1996 he chaired Wisconsin's Library Services and Construction Act Advisory Committee and was appointed by the Wisconsin State Legislature to the Joint Legislative Council's Special Committee on Public Libraries. Also in 1996, McMillan Memorial Library was honored by the secretary of the Smithsonian Institution for the Library's outstanding tradition of hosting traveling exhibitions. Mr. McCabe assisted Sarah Ann Long in developing her 1999-2000 American Library Association theme "Libraries Build Community." He served on the Public Library Association's Allie Beth Martin Award Jury in 1999 and 2000.